STEPPING STONES TO GRIEF RECOVERY

edited by
Deborah Roth

The Center for Help in
Time of Loss

IBS PRESS
Santa Monica, California

STEPPING STONES TO GRIEF RECOVERY
by The Center For Help in Time of Loss

Edited by Deborah Roth

Library of Congress Catalog Card Number: Pending
International Standard Book Number: 0-9616605-2-X

Published by IBS Press
744 Pier Street
Santa Monica, CA
tel: (213) 450-6485

Printed in the United States of America
First IBS PRESS Printing, May 1988

Note: this book originally appeared under the title *The Promise of
Green in the Season of Grief*.

Carvings in the Canyon, words and music by Barbara Meislin
and Amanda McBroom, Purple Lady Publishing—McBroom
Music/Careers.

*To Russ Ball
who built the boat, helped us into it,
and kept us afloat.*

ACKNOWLEDGMENTS

We are most grateful to Altrusa, a professional women's group in New Jersey, for the sponsorship of this project and to BG-888, another generous friend who was willing to help with the birth of this book.

For her editorial expertise, we owe a special debt of gratitude to Lynn St. Clair Strong, a "book doctor" who made many late-night housecalls. Many thanks also to Emily LeVier for her typing, patience and moral support, and to Joan Metzger, Susan Seligman and Grace Wohn for their constancy to the Center's work.

We wish to thank Mary O'Brien and her grandchildren: Mary Catherine, Maureen, Kathleen, Michael, Colleen and Suzanne who taught us the true meaning of loving support.

Finally, we wish to recognize all those people who have shared their lives with the Center and those who continue to join in healing.

CONTENTS

FOREWORD

It is with great pleasure that I write the foreword to this book. I have often asked the director of the Center to lecture on its program in order that other organizations and people could learn from the work this valuable facility is doing, specifically to learn how people suffering from the difficulties in life have helped others who are suffering similar pains. I have seen the Center support many individuals in their struggle with loss so that they could dare to take the next step in the living process and go on with their lives.

The Center offers no formulas or easy recipes. Nor does this book, which is written not by so-called "experts" with long lists of degrees but by people who have felt the pains of loss—who have not just studied them but lived them. This is not to say they don't listen to professionals; they do, but they have learned that eventually they will have to do the work themselves. Their stories make me think of a quote I read years ago in which the author (I believe it was attributed to Sigmund Freud) pointed out that often, when an individual dies, only good words are spoken about the deceased and suggested that this might be because none of us can help but admire the courage it takes to stand up to life. The people in this book confirm what extraordinary courage we "ordinary" human beings have.

From their experiences has come a set of guidelines or stepping stones to lead us through grief. All of those who contributed to these guidelines agree that no one can tell other people how to deal with their problems. They believe that each of us has a unique struggle. They will tell you that the journey is not easy. But they have found that by not running from difficulties there is a way to meet life's demands. They believe— no, they *know*—that this way works. They are an incredible support system.

Throughout this book, I sensed the presence of the deep inner healer, so like the shaman of our ancient cultures. Shamans must know illness and pain personally and be willing to confront death. Only then can they be born anew and help others to heal. I am confident that readers will travel along with these "wounded healers" who appear in this book. I believe their stories represent a remarkable compilation of what all of us will at some time encounter in our lives. On the basis of my experience in this field, both academically at the C.G. Jung Institute in Zurich, and personally in my workshops across the country, and through counseling, I am certain that this book will touch many lives. I thank the Center for writing it.

Gregg Furth, Ph.D.
New York City
October, 1987

STEPPING STONES TO GRIEF RECOVERY

1. THE DECISION TO ASK FOR HELP

2. THE WILLINGNESS TO SHATTER

3. THE HOPE TO FIND A WAY THROUGH

4. THE HONESTY TO LOOK WITHIN

5. THE PATIENCE TO STICK WITH THE PROCESS

6. THE TRUST TO KEEP OPEN

7. THE GRATITUDE TO PASS IT ON

For everything there is a season, and a time for
   every matter under heaven:
A time to be born, and a time to die;
A time to plant, and a time to pluck up what is
   planted.

                                          3:1-2

For every matter has its time and way, although
   man's trouble lies heavy upon him.

                                          8:6

But he who is joined with all the living has hope . . .

                                          9:4

                              —Ecclesiastes

INTRODUCTION

"How am I going to get through this?"

"Will I ever feel better?"

These are the questions most people ask in the face of bereavement, life-threatening illness or acute loss of any kind. It is the purpose of this book to share our own answers to these questions—to share our experiences, and our strength and hope, and the stepping stones that led us out of the darkest season of our lives.

In a sense this is a "how-to" book written by a group of ordinary people who came together to help themselves and others tunnel their way through grief. What began in 1978 as a weekly support group has since developed into a community support center for those who need help in time of loss. Although the Center remains primarily a self-help organization, a unique relationship between layman and professional has flowered. Physicians, nurses, psychologists, social workers and the clergy serve as advisors, and professional counseling is available, In addition to receiving patient referrals from doctors and hospitals, the Center offers an accredited six-week nurse's training course on working with the terminally ill and their families, and universities place graduate students at the Center for credit toward a master's degree in nursing.

The Center has developed a program that has already helped several thousand families in their recovery and healing. "Recovery" and "healing" may not seem totally fitting here, since some people who come to the Center have only a short time to live, but this is their story as well. What we learned from one another is how to live each day.

We also learned that each of us had to find our own answers. If we were willing to confront the most basic questions about loss, we would eventually discover what worked for us as individuals. We tell of our quests in the chapters ahead—our personal experiences and what we found together that helped us to heal. Because loss affects not only those in grief but everyone around them, we have included a chapter on ways to comfort the bereaved.

This is our response to the question "How will I get through this?" To the question "Will I ever feel better?" we can only answer for those of us who have been in that barren place. When we were sure that nothing would ever grow or bloom in our lives, that spring would never come again, together we found the promise of green.

> *In the deserts of the heart*
> *Let the healing fountain start.*
> *—W. H. Auden*

REACTIONS TO LOSS

You are not alone. Because grief can be so painful, and seem overwhelming, it frightens us. Many people worry if they are grieving in the "right" way, and wonder if the feelings they have are normal. Of course, there is no "right" way to grieve, and we encourage you to accept your feelings as natural. If you are concerned or worried about your reactions you may want to seek counseling. But it may help you to know that most people who suffer a loss experience one or more of the following:

Feel tightness in the throat or heaviness in the chest.

Have an empty feeling in their stomach and lose their appetite.

Feel restless and look for activity but find it difficult to concentrate.

Feel as though the loss isn't real, that it didn't happen.

Sense the loved one's presence: like finding themselves expecting the person to walk in the door at the usual time; hearing their voice; or seeing their face.

Wander aimlessly and forget or don't finish things they've started to do around the house.

Have difficulty sleeping, and dream of their loved one frequently.

Experience an intense preoccupation with the life of the deceased.

Assume mannerisms or traits of their loved one.

Feel guilty or angry over things that happened or didn't happen in the relationship with the deceased.

Feel intensely angry at the loved one for leaving them.

Feel as though they need to take care of other people who seem uncomfortable around them by politely not talking about their feelings of loss.

Need to tell, retell and remember things about the loved one and the experience of their death.

Feel their mood changes over the slightest things.

Cry at unexpected times.

These are all natural and normal grief responses. It's important to cry and talk with people when you need to.

1

Mary's Story

We can easily forgive a child who is afraid of the dark; the real tragedy of life is when men are afraid of the light.

—Plato

On the day after Thanksgiving, 1978, a group of people gathered at my house in River Vale, New Jersey, to ask if maybe there wasn't a better way to get over the rough places in life. Among the twenty-eight men and women in my living room that day, many were in the caring professions—doctors, nurses, a youth minister, several counselors and teachers. Others were there because they'd lost a loved one. At least six of the group had recovered from life-threatening illnesses of their own, and I was one of them.

What led me to call the meeting had really begun seventeen years earlier on a bleak October afternoon in 1961. My whole family was at our home for a party after my brother Pat's wedding. I was in my late twenties then, married to my childhood sweetheart, Russ. We had five children. Looking back, I guess I was still very much my parents' daughter, or, more precisely, "Daddy's girl." I adored my father. Everyone did. He was a dominating kind of man, but at the same time he was gentle and caring with a wonderful sense of humor. His law office was always filled with clients who most often couldn't pay their legal fees. I admired his principles and the ease with which he expressed his feelings. He had a hearty laugh, but he could cry, too, and no one felt embarrassed when he did. My father's greatest gift, I think, was his talent for listening, and because he had been raised by women he was particularly understanding of them.

I remember dressing up for a date and asking if he thought I looked okay. "Lovely, Sparky," he had said, using one of his pet names for me (the other was "Acoushla"). "But it's not your hair or clothes that matter. A woman's greatest assets are her eyes and her voice. Make sure you think before you speak."

I don't recall my father looking tired at the party that day, but suddenly he turned quite pale and complained about chest pains. When they took him to the hospital, I stayed behind with the children. A wash of fear came over me as I watched the car pull out of the driveway. I had the feeling I'd never see him again. Four hours later, he was dead. It was a heart attack. That strong, healthy, handsome man was gone—just like that.

After the initial shock and the brief flurry of after-funeral condolences, my mother went to visit her brother in California and my husband went to Washington, D.C., to look for work. Russ is a builder, and with little construction going on in the Northeast, and five small children, we were feeling the financial pressure.

A few months after my father's death, I found myself pregnant with a sixth child, a car that didn't work, and the feeling that I was very much alone. Even though I'd grown up in a Catholic household, watching

4

the priests come and go since I was little, it never occurred to me to seek help. At that moment I only wanted the father who had lived out on Long Island, but he wasn't there to help me anymore. So I just moped around with a heavy weight on my chest—that is, until one evening. I was about to feed the children when I decided to pour myself a drink, something I never did. Maybe it would make me feel better, I thought. It did just that—it masked my grief. From then on, I made it a habit at five o'clock to take a couple of drinks just to relax while I fed the children. In two months, I was drinking "round the clock." When our youngest daughter was born, I remember the shame I felt when the nurse told me there was alcohol on my breath and that I'd better cut out the drinking. I couldn't. I didn't know anything about alcoholism then. I didn't know it was a disease rather than a defect in my character.

For six years I couldn't stop, and I grew sicker by the minute. By the end of 1966, I was down to eighty-five pounds—thirty-five pounds less than my normal weight. My clothes and my hair were a disgrace, and as for what my father considered my best assets, my eyes were bloodshot and my voice was a raspy whisper. Our family doctor, who was about to throw up his hands, was deeply concerned about our six children. I was literally dying—and at my own hand.

That was when something stepped in and did for me what I could never have done for myself. Actually, it was as if I were hovering above my hospital bed, watching the medical team as they tried to revive me. I observed that my face was as white as the pillow, but I was completely detached emotionally. In fact, I had an indescribable sense of freedom and peace, with no desire to return to my body. But then I heard my doctor say, "We're going to lose her," and I thought, "I can't die—I have six children. Who's going to take care of

5

them?" And then, *zap,* just like that, I was back in my body. I have since read of similar experiences of people who have "died and come back," and all of them described feelings of peace and freedom. That experience took away my fear of death.

Not too long after I came home from the hospital, another incident occurred that I can only call a "spiritual experience." Russ and I were having dinner at my father-in-law's and I was sitting at the dining room table in my usual foggy stupor, pushing my food around the plate. Suddenly, something hit me with a great physical force, almost as if a cork were being forced out of a bottle—only I was the bottle. Some time later I described the experience to a priest (physical pain, the image of a man beckoning to me through the screen door, the feeling that I was dying), and he told me simply, but convincingly, that I had had a "deliverance from alcohol." I might wonder about the events, but I couldn't question the fact that my obsession to drink was gone as suddenly as it had come. I didn't want that obsession back, and, with the help of some people who showed me how to stay sober one day at a time, I haven't had a drink since August 1967.

It did take a good few years to repair the physical and emotional damage to myself and my family, but we made it back. Like any family with six children, we had more than our share of crises, including my own cancer scare: a lump in the breast turned out to be an encapsulated tumor requiring only surgery. We seemed to be well on our way to healing. Then my mother fell and broke her hip. She was on the critical list, and suddenly all my old fears were back again. I couldn't ignore the volcano rumbling inside me.

The fact is, I had come a long way, but I had never really faced the issue of loss. What I did know with certainty was that this time I needed help. Someone told

6

me about a "death and dying" group led by a therapist in a local hospital and I signed up immediately, but after one session I knew something was wrong with the approach. The atmosphere was judgmental and full of confrontation. The therapist seemed uncomfortable with any display of feelings, and he was forever pointing his finger at someone or stopping people when they cried. I had the feeling that we needed to release our emotions, not keep the lid on them. What was the matter with expressing despair, or anger, if that's how you felt?

Most of the people in the group were there because they'd lost a loved one, but a few were there because they were sick themselves. I heard them talk about their grief, and suddenly I knew what I had been feeling. It was grief. My mother was still alive, but her personality had begun to change during her illness and I felt I had lost the person I knew. I needed to be angry and cry my tears. I did get at least that much from the group—a growing confidence that trying to suppress grief wasn't natural and wouldn't work.

What I also got from the group was my first introduction to Dr. Elisabeth Kübler-Ross. Someone had brought in an article about her work with dying patients, and when I read it a breath of fresh air swept through that fear-filled room. I was excited by her philosophy. It was simple, and seemed to be true. This doctor just listened, without trying to tell people how it was for them. Her purpose was to learn from the patients—not to change them, but to support them however they were feeling. If they were angry, she listened; if they wanted to deny their circumstances, she didn't try to change their minds. What she was saying was that feelings aren't right or wrong; they just are. Someone had finally dared to say the emperor wasn't wearing any clothes, that dying was a fact of life and that not talking about it didn't make it go away. I had discovered that not talking about it could literally kill you. But who could you talk to about it? Even my husband, whom I could talk to about anything, seemed uneasy with the subject.

I wrote to Dr. Kübler-Ross, asking if she knew of a nonconfrontational group in my area that followed her philosophy. Elisabeth (as the doctor usually preferred to be called) wrote back that if I wasn't happy with what was available, maybe I should start my own group. But how could I, when I didn't have any credentials? She didn't see that as a problem. In fact, her response to that was: "Terrific, you won't have anything to un-learn."

Elisabeth wouldn't even connect me with anyone in my locale. She felt that if I was meant to do this, I should go off on my own and try it. "See how people relate to you," she said, "since that is what this work is all about."

It was the end of 1977, and on the evening of the "death and dying" group's final meeting I found my first contact. I had come home glad that the six weeks of frustration were finally over. (Always persistent, even when I didn't like something, I had finished out the ses-sions.) Sitting down that night with the newspapers, I spotted an article that started me thinking. It was a story about a young man who was teaching the first course on death and dying in the county, and it men-tioned that he was using Kübler-Ross' books as a guide. I decided to get in touch with him and anyone else I could find who followed her philosophy. I began scanning the papers. I found a six-week lecture series given by a pastoral counselor who had studied with Elisabeth, and I signed up for it. I called hospitals, con-tacted nurses and found out about a new hospice. In no time, I was a hospice volunteer. As the circle wid-ened, I met a young sociologist with a Ph.D. who was giving a course called "Death, Dying, Challenge and Change." He would eventually ask me and others from our new group to share our experiences with his class. He would also provide a weekly meeting place for us.

Elisabeth's work and her first book, published in the late sixties, had begun to change people's attitudes about dying. It was as if she'd given us permission to talk about feelings long held taboo, especially when the Fountain of Youth and facelifts had become modern idols. A ground swell had definitely begun; not one person I approached turned me down.

Elisabeth came to town, and we met. When I told her about the positive response, she said: "You'd better come to California for one of my workshops." It was less a statement than a command. My mother had begun to recover, and my family was very supportive, so off I went.

At Elisabeth's workshop in Escondido, I met many people who were facing their own death, some who worked with terminal patients and others who had recently lost a loved one. I wasn't sure what would come out of it, but I wanted to find out how I could help other people.

What I learned at the workshop was that you can't be effective while you're still filled with fears—that you need to get rid of your own debris before you're clear enough to help someone else. There were about seventy-five of us at the workshop, and as we shared our tears I heard Elisabeth say that we weren't crying for anyone but ourselves. Suddenly, I knew why it touched me so deeply when I heard someone cry over the loss of a child. It had triggered the memory of the stillbirth and the miscarriages I'd gone through many years before. I had pushed down my feelings then, and now they were surfacing.

There seemed to be a lot of the past that I hadn't let go of yet. I think all of us at the workshop found ourselves crying tears we didn't know we had. It wasn't morbidity; it was a different level of consciousness. The lids were off and the masks were gone. What made it all right—a relief, in fact—was the supportive atmosphere. Nobody gave advice or even reached out to anyone else. We were all just allowed to be who we were in a place that was safe.

Still, on my last night there, I began to wonder how far I was really willing to go with this. Was I ready to make a commitment—to devote my energy and time to starting a group? We roomed in a sort of commune setup, and I needed to be alone to think this through, so I found a large closet and pulled my sleeping bag inside. Before falling asleep I sent up a kind of prayer, asking if this was what I was really supposed to do. When I woke up the next morning, I could actually feel a pulse in the room. There were no voices, just a steady, almost audible rhythm. I am part of this heart-beat of humanity, I thought, and that was all the answer I needed.

"What do I do now?" I asked Elisabeth.

"You'll have to come back and work on yourself some more," she said.

I returned a month later for six weeks and followed Elisabeth around, watching how she was with patients. I liked what I saw. She was warm and caring, and the patients reached out to her like thirsty people in a desert. She didn't say much. She listened with compassion and without judgment.

One of the extraordinary people I met out there was a young woman who had cared for her dying child at home. She lived in my area, so I asked her if she'd be part of this new group I was starting. She was one of the people who gathered in my living room on that golden November afternoon. We were an odd lot, I thought, looking around the room—a mixture of ages, religious beliefs, educational and financial back-grounds. What we had in common was a desire to jour-ney to a dark and fearful continent known as death and loss. Elisabeth Kübler-Ross had been the explorer and pioneer. Up to this point, most of us had been talking about her discovery, studying her maps and teaching courses on the territory. Now a small band of people in a suburban ranch house were about to make a settle-ment in the new world.

I could hear the coffeepot perking above the friendly chatter as I stood to open the meeting. On the day after Thanksgiving, 1978, I had an inkling of how the Pilgrims must have felt just before the *Mayflower* set sail.

2

An Overview of Grief

We are healed of a suffering only by experiencing it to the full.

—Marcel Proust

$\mathcal{B}$y the time I had a chance to see the results of that meeting in Mary's living room, four years
had passed. My name is Debby, and my first encounter
with the Center came in the late summer of 1982 when
a friend's son was badly burned in a camping accident.
We didn't know if twelve-year-old Raymond would pull
through, yet I felt an immediate sense of calm and re-
assurance when his mother and I stopped at the Center one day on our way to the hospital. While everyone
there seemed genuinely concerned, I noticed an ab-
sence of fear. I was curious, and in the next six months,
as Raymond began to recover, I started raising questions about this support network that had eased the
trauma on his family.

"Why don't you help us define what we do," Mary
suggested, and that's how I got involved writing their
brochures and newsletters. I never expected the profound impact the Center would have on my life. Actually, it took almost five years for me to realize that I was

very much a participant in a common human experience, something I'd fought against ever since I can remember. Somewhere along the line, I'd gotten the idea that feelings were what other people "indulged in." I'd taught myself early on that I was "special" and that I could just figure it all out and not have to suffer the way other people did.

Trying to rise above it all, I see now, is a trick we play on ourselves. It allows us to feel momentarily superior and is a surefire way to develop a massive case of resentments. Being "noble" while everyone else is being human gets to be an awful drag. What psychology refers to as repression (more commonly called "stuffing your feelings") not only keeps you separate and isolated but can get you into a whole lot of trouble. You can keep things on ice for a very long time, but comes the thaw and there's apt to be a flood.

For me, that flood didn't happen for a long time. Not that I was a stranger to loss: I'd been through a divorce and a life-threatening illness; in fact, I was at the Center when the call came in that my father had just died. For a few years, I'd seen and written about people in grief, but I'd never really identified with them until two years after my father's death, when a relatively minor incident cracked my reserve and the dam broke. Several family problems had arisen at once, and I was feeling a little overwhelmed by them. I'd always assumed the role of helper, and it had never occurred to me to question why I should be the "family savior." But this time I was feeling resistant, so I discussed the issues with a counselor at the Center. When I mentioned one family member specifically, he said, "I don't know what you're going to do with *your* feelings, but right now hers are more pressing."

I didn't feel the rage until later. I wanted to shout, "My feelings are just as important as everyone else's!"

16

I had sat at the side of the pool for far too long, watching other people dive into the water. Now and then I'd stick a toe in to see how it felt, but now it was my turn. I couldn't help but acknowledge the turmoil inside, and for the first time I recognized that what I was feeling was a deep sense of grief.

COMMON REACTIONS TO LOSS

As I'd always suspected, being human isn't easy—but fighting it is worse. If you're fully alive and you love, there doesn't seem to be any way to avoid the pain of loss. And yet, when it happens, nobody's prepared. At the onset of a traumatic event, Nature, being kind and practical, temporarily numbs us. But when the natural anesthetic wears off, then what?

Overwhelmed by feelings, we're knocked off balance. We feel guilty, or angry, or hostile, and somewhere underneath we're afraid. And there's a physical response, too: a tightness in the throat, a heaviness in the chest. There's a feeling of emptiness in the stomach, but we have no appetite. We fluctuate between restlessness and profound fatigue.

There's also an urgent need for relief. Too often drugs or alcohol, or some other form of escape like overwork or shopping sprees, may look like a quick answer—anything to keep us too busy to think or feel. It's hard to concentrate. The idea is to keep moving, yet no place feels comfortable. When the pain sneaks up and there's no escape route, we may become temporarily paralyzed or wonder if we're "going crazy" or even harbor thoughts of suicide.

At the other extreme, we not only acknowledge but hold on to the pain—often feeling bitter and resentful.

In many instances we try to maintain our calm, appearing unaffected to others, maybe because way back we got the idea that it isn't appropriate to show feelings or because we're not quite ready to feel anything yet.

All these reactions, and more, may be part of grief. Of course, none of us is exactly like any other, and there is no neat checklist of responses. Still, it's reassuring to know that there are certain common patterns; indeed, various stages of grief have been noted. *Denial* of the event, *anger, bargaining* (or "making a deal with God"), *depression* and, finally, *peace and acceptance* are the five phases observed by Dr. Elisabeth Kübler-Ross in her work with dying people. In the booklet "Good Grief," Lutheran clergyman Granger Westberg divided the reactions into *shock, panic, resentment, resistance to returning to a normal life* and, as the final step to recovery, *affirmation of reality*. And from an academic viewpoint, Erich Lindemann, a professor of psychiatry at Harvard, classified the five most common symptoms of acute grief as *somatic* (or bodily) *distress, preoccupation with images of the deceased, guilt, hostile reactions* and *loss of patterns of conduct.*

Those who made these observations were quick to point out that not everyone goes through all the stages, that some might skip over one phase and return to it later, or vacillate between them. There are any number of variations.

A TIME TO GRIEVE

It can be comforting to know that our feelings are normal, but apparently what we do with these feelings can make or break our future. According to a study on the impact of loss featured in the New York *Times* in November 1985, people who do not work through the process of grief are liable to "suffer severe, long-term physical and emotional disturbances." The report indicated that psychologists were seeing delayed reactions to trauma in symptoms of sleeplessness, depression, and in some cases, even "distortions of the ability to work and love." These symptoms sometimes showed up years after the initial event.

Researchers have begun to suspect that unresolved grief is often the hidden culprit behind many of the complaints heard in doctors' offices and on psychiatrists' couches. Yet all of the literature tells us that grief is a natural process, part of being human. Obviously, something is "messing with Mother Nature."

Dr. C. G. Jung's response was that people all over the globe are resistant and unwilling to grieve: the Eastern part of the world tries to brush death off by calling it an illusion, and we in the West attempt to run away from it. But there is no way around loss, Jung said, and the only way to overcome it is by going straight through. The question is how.

What we're usually expected to do is muddle through on our own. Friends tell us that time heals all wounds, and then encourage us to get on with it. And we try, hoping that some of our former methods will work, because loss, after all, is no stranger to anyone. From the moment we come into the world, we lose the safe environment of the womb. As we grow up, we face a myriad of losses: a bicycle that's stolen, a pet that dies, a job or a relationship that doesn't work out, a jaw line that begins to sag. "Th .t's life," we tell ourselves, and somehow we manage to keep going. When each loss reminds us of our vulnerability, we seek a substitute to make us feel better, more secure: a new bike, a new pet, a new job or relationship, a face lift. If we feel a twinge now and then about our survival, well, what's the use of dwelling on it?

And then, suddenly, comes the loss for which there is no substitute, a loss that seems to shatter our lives. If we try to continue on as before, to "brave it out," relying only on time to heal us, we are liable, the experts caution, to feel the repercussions later. In fact, Dr. Robert Stevenson, one of the founding members of

19

the Center, who has since received his Ph.D. in thanatology, points out: "If we don't let nature take its course through us, we can end up with heart ailments, strokes or other serious disorders." The warning signs keep flashing: the escape route is hazardous.

ANOTHER CHOICE

Those who share their stories in these pages took another route and found that it led to recovery. At some point, each one decided that there might be a better way to heal and that maybe it wasn't necessary to go through grief alone. Their journeys are each unique, and each person is quite different in background and temperament. All are representative of everyone who has come to the Center. Like most of us, they were certain that they were different—that nobody had ever felt just as they did. To be sure, their circumstances differ, but as we've learned over time the nature of the loss is not always the best barometer for measuring its impact. A life-threatening illness of our own or a loved one, the death of a spouse, a parent or a child, a divorce or a job loss—each might rate a specific percentage on the psychologist's stress chart, but there seemed little benefit to be gained from entering a pain-judging contest. Nor was there much comfort in adages like "I cried because I had no shoes, until I saw a man who had no feet." Why should anyone be expected to feel better simply because someone else is in worse pain? Using similar logic, an irreverent newscaster on an old *Saturday Night Live* television show announced: "Today on the East Side a senseless killing took place, while on the West Side there was a sensible killing." When it comes to death or loss, comparisons just don't seem to work.

Eventually, special groups did develop at the Center because it was helpful for widows and widowers to share common experiences and for cancer survivors or burned people and their families to get together to discuss mutual problems and solutions. Parents who had lost children seemed to need special support in a peer group of their own. But in the long run it proved more helpful to identify with what others were feeling than to compare differences. We found that we could respect each other's uniqueness and still share a common goal: to help ourselves and others recover from loss.

ASKING THE RIGHT QUESTIONS
No one at the Center pretends to have the answers for anyone else, but we do offer support and encourage people to ask questions that will unlock their own answers. Some of the most commonly asked questions are raised in the chapters ahead, along with some of the answers that we've come up with.

One thing we've learned is that the best support is *not* advice giving. For that matter, the last thing someone in grief seems to need is to be told *how* to feel. We can, however, share our experience, strength and hope. We can say, for instance, that most of us found the year after loss the hardest because we had to face many "firsts" alone and each special occasion seemed to reopen the wound. Most often it takes from one to five years to integrate all the changes that have taken place. Some of us "got stuck" at some stage of recovery and found that professional counseling was helpful to getting back on the track. Becoming a truly whole human being is a monumental task—maybe the master task of a lifetime. Charles Lochner, coordinator of counseling services at the Center, explains it this way: "All of us, no matter how together we may seem, have broken places inside that cause us pain. When we dare to own those places and to acknowledge our struggle, we help ourselves and other people to relax a

21

bit and we ease the way." In cases where loss triggers some unresolved grief from the past, or causes some deeper underlying problem to surface, more extensive therapy is often suggested; but grief counseling at the Center is almost always short-term, which means that it generally lasts no longer than a year.

As more and more people have come to the Center to embark on their grief work, we've watched the process of healing take place. We've seen people discover resources they didn't know they had and recover their balance so they could begin to function again. Many who were once hopeless, and thought they could never come to terms with what had happened, found a way to accept the unacceptable. And some found more. Those who chose to use the period of grief as a jumping-off place from which they could go on to explore long-held beliefs about death and life came upon a few surprises. Many found a new, less fearful way to relate to other people and to the world.

Although grief work seems to take place mostly on an inner level, sometimes a practical approach is crucial to going through the difficult, piercing moments. What do you do at five o'clock when no one is coming home for dinner, or at three when you hear the laughter of children getting off the school bus and your child is no longer among them?

People at the Center who have lived through these moments approach the acute pain in various ways. Some have changed their normal routines so that they would not have to confront these times alone, while others have made the deliberate choice to sit still and experience them. Their stories tell how they handled the immediate impact of loss, and some suggestions from a professional are offered in Chapter Seven. When it comes to specifics, most of us have our own solutions, but over the years we began to see that there are certain common markers on the road to recovery. What we've come to call the Seven Stepping Stones are detailed in the next chapter.

PROMISES

Having followed many individual journeys to the outcome, we've grown bold enough to make two promises. First, those who choose to take the road through grief will sooner or later come to a gentler place and they *will* feel better. Second, for those who allow themselves special nurturing, like plants brought inside against a sudden frost, healing will take place. In their own time and season, a new form of life will appear— and "the promise of green" will be fulfilled.

3

The Heart of the Matter

It is then that you will hear a voice within yourself.
It was there all the time, but you never
listened before.
Faintly it will speak to you at first,
But it will gradually grow louder and clearer
the more you take heed of its message
Until it thunders inside you and you will have come
home.

—Kristin Zambucka

$\mathcal{W}$e believe that people in grief do best in a safe place where they can come and listen to themselves and where they can move toward recovery at their own pace, without being prodded or judged. The Center provides this safe place. In the turmoil of grief it's almost impossible to sort through our thoughts and feelings, but when we take the time to hear what's inside us, without rushing to fix things or make ourselves feel better right away, something remarkable happens. A natural intelligence appears to take charge. This faculty, closer to common sense than to intellect, is more a knowing than knowledge and has been alluded to by poets and philosophers throughout the ages. George Santayana, for instance, touched on it when he wrote: "It is not only wisdom to be wise, and on the inner vision close the eyes, but it is wisdom to believe the heart."

In our own experience, people gain confidence in

their ability to survive as they begin to trust their heart wisdom. They begin to thrive and grow.

STEPPING STONES TO RECOVERY

Our way, of course, is not the only one, but it works for us. You could say we travel mostly on foot, covering every inch of the terrain. We take no shortcuts or detours around our pain, and what sustains us is that we're not traveling alone.

Our route to recovery is marked by seven stepping stones:

1. The decision to ask for help
2. The willingness to shatter
3. The hope to find a way through
4. The honesty to look within
5. The patience to stick with the process
6. The trust to keep open
7. The gratitude to pass it on

Listing seven stepping stones by number, as if there were an orderly march through grief, might seem odd considering the uniqueness of each person's experience and the chaotic nature of the grieving period. In retrospect, however, we've found that there is an order to the process even though we can't see it at the time. While a significant loss may alter our lives permanently, the actual recovery period is a process with a beginning and an end. Paradoxically, the very sense of disorientation, of things being out of control, signals the beginning of the journey. Many people at the Center have described this sensation of being off balance. One woman said she felt wobbly, like a stool with one of its legs missing; a widower talked about being spun off from his center like a mad gyroscope.

Asking for help or emotional support at this time is alien to many people. Men seem to have a particularly difficult time reaching out at first, although women, too, put up a front, and try to stand on their own two feet when their legs are buckling. People who come to the Center have already touched the first stepping stone: *the decision to ask for help.*

Those in grief often talk about the turmoil they're in, but few, if any, are ready to surrender to the impact of loss. We believe *the willingness to shatter* eventually comes about only in a supportive atmosphere where people feel secure enough to "let go."

Those who come to the Center usually find *hope* when they see others plowing their way through similar circumstances, but not all of them choose to deal with their feelings in a prolonged way. Approaching the fourth stepping stone—*the honesty to look within*—is like confronting a closet jam-packed with the accumulation of years. It's a great temptation to shove one more thing inside, if possible, and put off the task of sorting it out.

Those who decide to stay and tackle the job find that it takes *patience* and *trust,* the next two stepping stones, to examine feelings, discard worn-out ideas and develop new perceptions that lead to lasting comfort and healing.

It's not uncommon for some to bypass the process and head straight for stepping stone seven by offering help to others before they've helped themselves. In our experience, the most successful professionals and volunteers are those who are willing to work through their own healing and then *pass it on*. This is why we use the word "gratitude" in the final step. It refers to a gift already received. In fact, a study conducted at the Center in 1985 showed that the volunteers who stay the longest and display the greatest commitment are those who wish to share what they've received, while those who seek chiefly to console themselves by helping others tend to drop out of volunteering in a relatively short time. Healing from loss, not unlike a physical healing, seems to take place from the inside out.

SETTING OUT

Where does this journey begin? At whatever point the choice to recover is made. A total belief in recovery is not required. Doubts are bound to come and go, but the setting of a goal at the beginning establishes the direction to be taken. And isn't it true, whether we acknowledge it or not, that we always make some choice about what we want?

People who believe that feeling better would demean a loved one who died, or that it would somehow dishonor their relationship to that person, might find it impossible to make a commitment to recover until the feelings of guilt are resolved. A woman who had lost her young son, for instance, found that she was torn by guilt whenever she began to feel the slightest relief from her suffering. "I wondered what kind of a person I was," she said, "to feel at peace when my child would never enjoy life again." She realized that she was trapped by the conflict, and her awareness made a choice possible—if not right away, at least when she was ready.

Recovery may also have different meanings for those in grief. Take, for example, the elderly widower who stopped by the Center during a visit from Spain. His beloved wife had died fifteen years earlier, he told us, "and I've never looked at another woman since." He spoke poignantly of his memories, but his vitality and humor were ample evidence that he had healed in his own way. The form is of little consequence. Recovery may include many new relationships, remarriage or remaining as the gentleman from Barcelona did. What matters is the desire to mend.

Those who reach out for help have already displayed that desire. So where do you begin? Right here.

And where are you going? Counselor Charles Lochner, says it best: "We are each on a journey to our own heart."

GOING GENTLY

The single most important feature of this journey, we believe, is self-compassion. It has become popular to speak about loving yourself, but the meaning of that phrase is often obscure. Conditioned as most of us are to refraining from being self-centered, and cautioned against self-pity, we may find it difficult to exercise one of our most important rights: the right to self-concern.

Grief requires that we take ourselves seriously. With others prodding us to move along quickly, it takes real strength to be gentle with ourselves. Perhaps the most essential lesson to be learned from grief is the fine art of caring for ourselves with compassion—to have patience with ourselves, to be who we are at the moment even if we don't like what we are feeling.

Dr. Theodore Rubin, in his book *Compassion and Self-Hate*, discusses the harsh treatment people unknowingly inflict on themselves in their quest for perfectionism. He talks about how our unrealistic demands on ourselves can stunt our growth and rob us of living fulfilled lives. He encourages us to fight for our right to make mistakes, to appear foolish, to be human. Those of us who are going through the all-too-human experience of grief can well use such encouragement.

IN THE COMPANY OF OTHERS

No other experience is quite so isolating as grief. Pain makes us feel separate and seems to set up a barrier between ourselves and other people. Communication breaks down, and even those who are closest to us have difficulty finding their way in. They try to comfort us, but after a while they may grow impatient because we simply cannot move along at a normal pace. Since many people are deeply disturbed by loss, our experience may frighten them. Besides, when we are grieving we need to talk about what has happened to us, sometimes repeating ourselves over and over again. We don't expect other people to listen endlessly, so we're apt to remain silent or mask our feelings.

At the Center our answer to this sense of isolation is support groups, where people have the opportunity to express themselves in a way they cannot do out in the world. Support groups are not for everyone, so we ask people who come to the Center to make a six-week commitment to determine if the process is suitable for them. We suggest that people wait until two or three months after a loss before coming. By then the shock has usually dissipated and the process can be utilized more fully. For those in immediate need, one-to-one counseling is available.

Newcomers are asked to attend an orientation a half-hour before group, and the following is what we usually say:

"If you really listen to yourself and give yourself permission to be who you are at this moment in time, you'll get out of the program exactly what you put into it. You'll begin to know yourself.

"This is how it works: The moderator, who might have been working in a group last week and who may be a participant next week, will open the session. There are no bosses here, only people who have been through a loss of their own and who have begun to get better. The moderator may read a poem or an inspiring passage so that you can reflect on what brought you here. We use a round-robin format, and when it's your turn just allow yourself to say anything that comes up. You can express whatever feelings are present for you. You can hate God. You can hate the person you've lost. You can hate whatever is happening in your life. There's no cross-talk, no advice giving, no judgment.

"If you need to cry, nobody will stop you: nobody will touch you. It's like being wrapped in a magic circle. No one can reach over into your space. You can say anything, and no one outside the room will ever hear about it. That's what makes it a safe place. Whatever is said here, stays here.

"Tissues will be in the middle of the floor, within easy reach. If we handed them to you, you might stop and swallow your tears. In the world outside there's always a tendency for people to make a comforting gesture toward you when you're crying, which is really their way of stopping you. We allow you to cry.

"Sometimes it's as if there's a big lump inside you that needs to break and be released. There may be anger that needs to be released as well. Anger produces change, so if you're feeling that emotion you might beat your bed with a tennis racket when you go home, or jog or bang a tennis ball to get some of the feelings out.

"There's no easy way through pain. That's why many people say after group that they don't know if they can come back. It's kind of like having your appendix out. You don't look forward to the operation, but you know you'll be fine once it's over."

ON BEING A LISTENER

Listening to members of the group gives people the chance to look back on how it was for them in the past, and the newcomers get an idea of how it will be for them farther down the road.

One of the participants confided that she couldn't prevent her head from judging herself and everyone else. "I started comparing what I felt to everyone else's feelings," she said. "Sometimes I'd grow impatient.

33

But before long I began to see the effort people were making, and I couldn't help but admire the courage I saw. I found myself silently cheering them on."

When people can get past judgment, they feel less isolated and more able to relate to others. It's not easy to describe what really happens in group. A member of the group shared her impression of how it works in the following poem.

TO ALL OF YOU WHO LISTEN
I brought you my tears, like an angry child, and said
"Now make them stop." You wouldn't.
I brought you my fears, with trembling hands, and said
"Make them go away." You couldn't.
I brought you my rage, red and raw, and said,
"Make me feel better." You didn't.
I brought you my despair, dark and heavy, and said
"Do something about this!" You listened.

"Well," said I, "What good are you anyway? What do I need you for? I brought you my tears, my fears, my rage and my despair—and what did you do? Absolutely nothing. You did not do one single thing that I asked you to do. Why do I even come here? I had to do something about these things all by myself. All you ever did was sit around in a circle, week after week, and listen to me. And
listen to me!
And...
love me!
Week after week."

—Rona

4

Breakthrough

I warn you, if God gives you the grace to let go, get ready for an unexpected transformation.

—Macrina Wiederken, O.S.B.

One look at the stepping stones and you might wonder why anyone would want to consider a process that asks you to fall apart. Some cultures foster the recognition of grief (Orthodox Jews, for example, are expected to tear their garments during the mourning period), but overt expressions of deep emotion are rarely encouraged in our society. And if you've been brought up in the American tradition of "keeping a stiff upper lip" and "pulling yourself up by your bootstraps," the last thing you're prepared to do is come apart at the seams.

To make matters worse, giving in to grief can mean opening up the unknown. What if you break into a million pieces that can never be put back together again? "Nothing is healthier than a good nervous breakdown," they say, and "breakdowns mean breakthroughs," but that's pretty cold comfort when your own sanity is at stake. "Am I going crazy?" is the last thing you want to ask yourself, but in fact that's the question many of us ask in our grief.

Dottie's Story

It was a mother's worst nightmare—the thing you hope you won't dream about when you go to bed at night. It was such a horrendous piece of information that I could barely comprehend it: cancer . . . a certain kind of leukemia . . . a fifty-fifty prognosis.

How could this have anything to do with Jessie, my rambunctious little girl?

When she didn't feel well that spring, I'd thought maybe it was bronchitis or, at the very worst, pneumonia. Then I began to notice a swelling around the lymph nodes under her chin. It looked like mumps, but why was her belly so swollen? By Easter Sunday, I knew she was quite sick. I called the doctor, and he seemed to know what it was right away—that's how classic her symptoms were. He saw us that day, but then he sent us home to have Easter with the family.

"Don't let Jessie out of your sight," he said. "Something is very wrong with her, but we can't do anything until tomorrow anyway."

On Monday the blood tests were done, and Tuesday morning the doctor came into the hospital room with the diagnosis. I remember feeling like Dorothy in *The Wizard of Oz*—swirling, going round and round in a blur of needles and nurses. My husband had gone to class that morning (he was attending college back then), so the only one in the room with me was my father. We just looked at each other for a moment, then I put my head on his shoulder and we hung on to each other.

Over the next few days, I tried to get my bearings. I don't remember ever feeling so helpless. My marriage was already shaky by then, and I felt very much alone with Jessie's illness. What I needed was a sense of control. I'd have to get all the information I could about leukemia—some clear facts, something tangible to focus on.

When the results from the bone marrow, spinal tap and other tests were in, the figures went up to seventy percent chance for recovery. That gave me some hope. By then, Jessie had been transferred from New Jersey to a hospital in New York City. I can still see her in that iron crib with the lid on it and tubes coming out of her everywhere. With all the drugs they were administering, it seemed as though she'd been stuck a million times.

That's when I began hounding the staff. "You've got to give me a schedule of her medicine," I told them. "I want a list of her chemotherapy and a description of it." I discovered that no matter how many times I went over her regimen, I couldn't seem to absorb what I was reading. It took, I'd say, the whole two weeks we were there, constantly asking questions, to finally understand. The nurses were exceptional. They knew what the families were going through, and sometimes they'd sit up with me until three in the morning, explaining. Finally, it began to get through to me what a blood count meant, and the breakup, and that I could check the white cell count and the differential. And the doctor gave me an extraordinary piece of advice: "Write down everything she's supposed to have," he said. "You're the expert on the case. If you know she's due to have something at one o'clock and she hasn't had it, go out in the hall and find out why."

I began to keep a journal, a record of everything that happened down to the last detail. Who drew blood. At what time. Who came in and asked questions. What kinds of tests they did, and when. I saved Jessie from I don't know how many duplications and all the unnecessary agony that went with them.

39

I don't know what came over me, but something told me I had to be totally honest with Jessie. She had turned two in December, and this was only April, but I had the idea she could understand everything. I'm sure it was the right thing to do, because she needed to know that on a certain day it was going to be this or that procedure, and that nothing else would happen to her. I was absolutely adamant about people coming in and telling her what they were there for. "Tell her right away, and don't you make that child feel anxious while you sit there and make small talk," I told them. I think they must have had a not-so-nice nickname for me, but after a while, unless they were going to play with her, they would just get the procedure over with. There was none of that ambiguity that's so unnerving. I've seen the effect of that on other kids, when I went into their rooms and told them I just wanted to talk to their parents. They looked as if they didn't believe me.

A year or so into the treatment, Jessie developed toxicity to certain medicines. Her protocol for chemotherapy was technically once a month, but there were so many quirks that we usually ended up in the hospital once a week.

I was trying to do everything myself. We didn't have much of a normal life, but I tried to hold it together as best I could until that day I finally snapped. We were in the emergency room of our local hospital: Jessie and I, and my son Lee, who was six then. Jessie was scheduled for chemotherapy. It was our regular doctor's day off. Whenever that happened, the doctor would arrange for someone competent to take over so that I didn't have to worry. He must have forgotten that day, because no one at Emergency knew who we were. From the looks I got, they seemed to think I was out of my mind asking for such a horrendously powerful drug for the adorable baby girl who was smiling up at them. They refused to give it to me, and I was so frantic that I became practically incoherent. I couldn't hold back the tears. It seemed like hours that I just stood there crying, trying to explain what we wanted. There must have been ten or fifteen nurses and technicians standing around me. Suddenly, my son threw up his arms.

"Oh, my God," he said. "I knew it. She's drunk!"

All eyes in that room were on me. I imagined a lot of knowing winks and whispers. Now they must be convinced that I was the one that needed help. I was sure they were about to cart me away. Besides the fact that it was ten o'clock in the morning, I don't even drink, and there I stood looking like a candidate for the drunk tank or the mental ward.

That's when I began to wonder if I was going crazy. Jessica had been diagnosed in April of 1981, and that September my husband and I had separated. With all the problems in the marriage to begin with, the illness pushed it over the edge. I just didn't have the energy to cope with both. By April of '82, we were divorced. I never thought about going to a professional, because, well, in my family that was always taboo. To this day my grandmother will tell you, "I've been through more than anyone I know, and I never went to a psychiatrist." I wasn't used to relying on anyone. As the oldest of seven children, I had always been the mainstay—the one everybody else turned to. I just didn't know how to ask for help.

So it was a big step for me to say, gee, maybe I'm not okay. But I knew I had to do something. I saw an ad in the paper for the Center's support group, and I called. Mary must have heard the need in my voice. She told me all about the group and listened while my story tumbled out.

I remember my first time in group, hearing the

moderator say, "Just peel away the layers until you get to what's at the bottom." I started to cry and I realized I hadn't really allowed myself to let go for two years. Two years! At group I began talking out loud and hearing myself. I realized how incensed I was that nobody had recognized my need for help. I didn't want to be put on a pedestal or given a halo. I'm not a saint. The truth is, I was a nervous wreck. It seemed years since I'd had a conversation with anybody above the age of ten. My kids were driving me crazy. I couldn't pay the bills, and I was worried sick about Jessie. I didn't know whether to laugh, cry or scream. But for the first time I had found a place to say, "I can't do this anymore." I had a good chance to look at my feelings, and once I identified the anger, I felt better. It was *anger,* it was *legitimate,* and it was *okay.* I remember talking to someone outside group at the Center one day, and when I finally finished blowing off a little steam, she just looked at me and said, "You've had a rough time, haven't you?" I burst into tears because someone had acknowledged what I'd been through. I needed affirmation.

Every Tuesday I went to group like clockwork. It was as if someone had thrown me a lifeline and I was holding on to it for dear life. I marveled at the acceptance I felt. I was used to judgmental advice: "I know what your problem is, and what you should do." I didn't need that. I just needed a peaceful place to "unload," to talk it through and work it out. And that's what I'd found—people who didn't interrupt me, who weren't waiting for me to finish so they could put their two cents in. The Center was a place where I could cry until I was done crying. I cried, I'd say, for a year straight. Jessie was coming along nicely, but still I was uneasy about the future, and I was troubled about my son Lee and his feelings of guilt. I thought we'd worked through the problem, but he couldn't seem to shake the idea that he was responsible for Jessie's illness and for his father not living with us. No matter how hard I tried, I couldn't find a way to help him. Then someone at the Center suggested counseling—for myself rather than for Lee, who was already in the young people's support group—as a way for me to gain strength so I could help us both.

I discovered that I had a real "authority problem." Your relationship with doctors gets so out of proportion, because you feel like they hold your child's life in their hands. I went through every emotion from hating them to loving them to being afraid of them. That was one of the reasons I'd held myself in for so long. God forbid I'd cry, and then they would think I wasn't capable of handling Jessie's regimen. Every time I talked to them, I'd get all worked up and be unable to express myself until it was too late.

Between brief counseling and continuing with the group, I began to ease up on myself and find new confidence. The private sessions were immensely helpful, but I believe I owe the good place I'm in to the nonprofessionals, to people whose last names I didn't even know—people who came to group every week and loved me, and listened to me, and just let me be.

It's been an interesting evolution for me. I don't have this mind-reader mentality anymore. Now I say how I feel, and all my relationships have changed because of this. They've become more honest. That goes for my relationship with God, too. Week after week, seeing all those children in the hospital, made me question everything I believed. I know life happens to people, but I just couldn't understand why children had to suffer like this.

In time I began to let go of the "whys," and I've developed a different, I'd say closer, relationship with God. Now I tell *Him* how I feel. I'll say, "I'm really upset today, so please don't let anything else happen right now. I've had enough!" And I feel He understands. He's pushed me to my limit, and somehow I'm able to make peace with that. When Jessica first got sick, I went through a period of rebellion. I remember being furious when someone brought her a bottle of holy water from Lourdes. I was fed up with having people shove all that down my throat— "I'll pray this" or "You should pray that." First I took the bottle and put it on my dresser. Then I put a drop of the holy water on Jessie and put the bottle back on my dresser. It was a kind of defiance, like putting a statue of St. Jude on his head. It was like saying, "All right. So show me what you're gonna do!" Still, at the same time I can't forget the priest who helped me. He came to the hospital that first traumatic week when Jessie became ill. He came and brought me Communion. He said nothing. He didn't preach at me. He just hugged me, sat with me awhile and left. And that was what I needed from him.

I guess you could say that my faith has grown big enough to encompass all of it, the good and the bad. I seem to have accepted where the real authority lies, and this doesn't scare me the way it once did. Jessie seems to have no trouble with it at all. Sometimes I can hear her praying at night: "You know, God, there's people who are hungry. I hope you're gonna feed them. I don't want the mommies crying because their babies are hungry." She prays for all her friends from the hospital who have died and calls all the angels by name.

Sometimes I have to walk out of her room because I can't deal directly with some of the facts. But I have made a choice. I understand all the negative energy people feel, but for my own psychology, my own well-being, I have to turn the situation around to something positive. I have to make a difference. I have to stand up and shout until we make it better for children. I don't expect to change the world, but I think we can change some lives.

My labor of love is the Tomorrow's Children fund, which started in a hospital in New York City. I'm the director of it now. It's a parents' group that has added the human touch: a playroom, nutritious snacks for the kids, a coffeepot always perking for the adults. More important, we're raising funds, and the people we hire may one day find a cure. Now we're in a medical center in New Jersey, where the staff listens to us and really hears us. Even on a personal level, it's different. I had lunch with one of the doctors the other day, and it seemed natural that she would ask my advice—not on medical matters, of course, but when it comes to helping families cope, the doctors often talk things over with me. They know how much firsthand experience I've had. I'm much less intimidated now, since I'm at ease with myself.

A lot of good things have happened. Jessie is finished with chemotherapy, and it looks like she's out of the woods. I've remarried. I never would have believed that life could open up and take us on a completely new path.

Coming unglued was a frightening and terrible experience—beliefs, self-image, everything came apart—but I feel that my energy and whatever gifts and talents I have can be put to good use now. I don't believe we'd have come through the way we did if it hadn't been for the kind of support we received. I don't know how people go through the rough times without it.

5

A Conspiracy of Kindness

It takes two to speak the truth—one to speak, and another to hear.

—Henry David Thoreau

$\mathcal{I}$t isn't easy, when we're going through a loss, to find the right kind of emotional support. In a world where everyone is going about "business as usual," it can be very uncomfortable to grieve. Not only are other people awkward about offering solace, but we compound the problem by not wanting to embarrass them with too much emotion. Sadly, this means that they end up tiptoeing around our pain or saying the things we don't want to hear: "Well, you have your health," or "You have to go on for the sake of the children," or, least helpful of all, "Some people have it a lot worse!"

Feeling frustrated and even more alone, we may ask ourselves when this conspiracy of kindness will ever end. It took Holly, a young widow, almost seven years to do something about it.

Holly's Story

I wish I'd known about the Center a long time ago. Actually, I could have used support from the very moment

49

my husband was diagnosed. Right from the start I felt as though no one knew how to handle what was happening—and worse, no one was communicating with anyone else.

Don had developed a really terrible cough that spring, and by May I knew this was something more than just your basic cold. He had awful back pains, and pains in his legs, but he wasn't the type to go to a doctor and it wasn't until June that he finally went for a physical. We had one of those medical plans with the facilities all in one place and a physician assigned to you. Don was examined by a young, mild-mannered woman doctor. She started looking for muscle or spinal problems, because the pain in his back and legs was what had brought him to her. She did discover a small lump in his left armpit, but she decided not to do anything except follow it for any change. We had planned our vacation for the last three weeks in July and I expected her to tell us not to go, but she said not to worry—that there was no urgency.

Two days before we left for Hilton Head in South Carolina, we went to a friend's Fourth of July picnic. It was a glorious day except for a strange incident. Don was holding a fragile champagne glass, which dropped from his hand and shattered. Nobody paid much attention, but then it happened again. Don seemed to be losing the ability to do simple things. I knew something was very wrong, but he disagreed. A voice in my head told me, "This is not right," but a bigger voice said: "This is his body and I can't make him do anything about it."

A day or so after we arrived at Hilton Head, we were relaxing by the ocean when Don began pounding on the arms of his beach chair, fighting off the pain. I begged him to call the doctor and at least let her prescribe something for him, but he refused to cut short our vacation.

July was almost over by the time we came home and Don saw the doctor again. The lump under his arm had clearly grown larger, so she sent him to a surgeon that same day and he was scheduled for an exploratory the following morning. He didn't act at all worried—in fact, he seemed convinced that nothing was seriously wrong with him.

It was an early morning operation, and I got to the hospital around eleven when visiting hours started. No one had told me that I could have come earlier to be with him. Actually nobody spoke to me at all. The nurses behaved as if I weren't even there. Don's room was empty. I just sat there, not knowing what to do, until my uncle arrived. He was a volunteer at the hospital, and when he heard how long the operation had been going on, he went to see what he could find out. The only information he could get was that Don was in recovery and that the surgeon should be down any minute to talk to me. Another two hours went by and finally I went to the desk to see if someone could get hold of him. They tracked him down at his office, and when he eventually called me back at the nurses' station, all he said was: "It's very bad—it's what we call the black cancer." That was how I found out.

I was numb. I remember asking how long he thought we had, and he said he couldn't say because he didn't know. Only if I asked him a direct question would he tell me anything. He acted as if he couldn't have cared less. He was considered to be one of the leading oncology surgeons, the former head of his department. I'd say he was in his late sixties.

I went back into Don's room, and that was when I lost control. I just lay down on the empty bed and sobbed. Some time later, a nurse came in and asked if I was all right. When I said no, I wasn't, she handed me a box of tissues and left. My uncle came up again, and I told him about Don. I was glad to have somebody with me. My parents were away in Europe, and I didn't want my grandmother in Brooklyn to have to deal with this alone. My uncle ended up calling my sister for me, but I knew she was taking care of her young son at home and I wasn't sure she'd be able to get away. I was so grateful when she walked into the room a short time later. We sat together, not saying much, just holding hands.

When they brought Don down from recovery, I thought how glad I was that he still looked like himself. He was only in the room a few minutes when our doctor phoned to say that she'd spoken to the surgeon. She asked if I had told Don what they'd found. I wished that she had come and talked to us together. Now it was all on my shoulders, and I wasn't sure how to tell him.

When I got off the phone, Don asked, "What is it?"

I told him to rest awhile and when he was fully awake I'd tell him. "Tell me now," he said.

All I could say was: "Don, it's cancer."

I was glad the moment was over, but the look on Don's face—it was like a shrug. He gave up in that moment and I don't know why.

Everything happened so fast. On Wednesday I had no idea about cancer, by Thursday I knew I needed to know a lot. I called everyone who might fill me in. I began quizzing the oncology specialists who had just come on the case, and I became the interpreter between them and Don. None of the doctors held out much hope. They would pat my hand and say, "Isn't she cute to gather all this medical information," very patronizing or pitying, and I knew they'd given up on Don. His diagnosis was metastatic, malignant melanoma, and when the tests were in we learned that it was everywhere in his body.

What amazed me was that Don didn't *look* sick.

He looked pink and healthy and beautiful. Besides that, he had skin cancer yet nothing had appeared on his skin. Everything seemed out of whack. Here was this dying man who looked perfectly healthy.

On the day Don was discharged from the hospital and we had just arrived home, he said to me, "I'm doing the one thing you desperately didn't want me to do—dying!" But after that he was very closed. He wouldn't talk about what was happening unless he had to. Once when I was nestled next to him on the bed, I asked him about a memorial service. He said he wanted a cocktail party instead. I told him he'd probably like us to read some Mark Twain, and he said, yes, "Captain Stormfield's Visit to Heaven." That was the end of the discussion.

For a while Don and I still went to work, but usually he'd call me after twenty minutes or so and ask me to drive him home. I was running his business, doing my job, running the household and caring for him and Charlie, our six-year-old. Charlie was wonderful with his father. During Don's hospital stay, I remember coming into the room and seeing Charlie in the middle of Don's bed, eating chocolate ice cream as natural as could be, just waiting for his father to come down from a treatment. They had a gentle, easy way with one another. Don's other three children were the same way (Don was a few years older than I, and he'd been married before). I'd say all four of them were capable of dealing with the situation a lot more honestly than other people around me.

One day, I had lunch with a friend who said, "This must be a real seesaw for you." That was as close as any of my friends came to saying anything.

It was the worst of times and in some ways the best. It was the worst because of what Don was going through, but it was my job to take care of him, and I

53

think it was the best job I've ever done at anything. I made him comfortable and I made him laugh.

All along I'd been trying to get Don to do everything possible that might help. At one point, the oncologist in charge took me aside. "You've got to leave him alone," he told me. "You're pushing him when there's no reason to."

By the end of September, I began to wonder if he wasn't right. I was feeling overwhelmed with all the decisions about treatments. One morning in the shower, which has always been a private place—a place where I could pray, I asked what I should do. Suddenly, I heard this voice in my head say, "I am the only answer." I knew it was the voice of God and I knew it was true. It was in God's hands, so whatever happened would be the right thing to happen. It wasn't that I was religious; I hadn't practiced my religion since I'd left my parents' house. I was definitely a Jewish person with a belief in God. When I heard that voice it was a relief—somebody else was taking over. I think that was the moment I finally admitted to myself how much I really needed help. Not that my parents weren't supportive; they tried to help me deal with the practical day-to-day things, but they were terrified. They couldn't treat me as though I were about to become a widow, because that would mean acknowledging that Don was going to die.

In October, Don grew much weaker. One terrible night, the disease erupted in four different places in his brain. Don was no longer Don. He didn't know anybody was there; he was speaking gibberish and he was blind. When I called the doctor, he told me that it might be a reaction to the medicine. I kept calling back, telling him that we had to get this man to a hospital. It might have been easier if I'd known about Hospice, but nobody ever mentioned it. I remember Charlie had a stomach virus that night, and I kept running back and forth between him and Don, becoming more and more frantic.

It was six in the morning when the ambulance finally came. By then, Don was in a coma. When he came out of it at the hospital, all he could say was my name, over and over again.

I don't know how long I'd been sitting by Don's bed when a nurse motioned me into the hall. "You have to take care of yourself," she said. "You have to do something for you." All I could do was cry, and all she could do was put her arms around me. She's the only person who responded to me that way. She was just a nurse on the floor, but she had the affection and the courage to reach out to me.

Then it was November, and I was at home trying to get a little sleep when the nurse called to say it was over. I knew two things at that moment. One was that it wasn't Don's life that had ended, it was his dying. The other was that everybody's task had definitely been played out. Even if it wasn't the ending I wanted, it was done right.

It's been almost seven years now, and at last I think I'm beginning to really take that nurse's advice and do something for myself. I can't say I ever really gave myself time to grieve. Two weeks after Don's death, I took over his business and went to a convention in California because I was sure if I didn't everything would fall apart. I just kept going.

All the books say it should take a year or two to recover. I don't know if it takes two weeks or twenty years, and it's probably different for everyone, but I wonder—maybe it wouldn't have taken so long if I'd had the right support sooner. Going through it alone, I'd say I've done my grieving mostly in increments, letting go of the past in bits and pieces.

People talk about the stages of mourning; they don't talk about the stages of healing—that's what we should be looking for. Some of them are simple, like when you have gone several days and you haven't had constant thoughts about the person who died. When you realize there is pleasure in life as well as sadness, you know the healing is happening. You know you're better when the normal irritations begin to frustrate you. You're better when you get mad at the sales clerk for taking three people ahead of you. You're healing when you're back in the mainstream of life, finding pleasure and pain in other things than this one main event. When I can separate from it, and feel like it happened to another person, then I think I'll be healed. It doesn't feel that way yet, but I can feel the edges. There is also a part of me that wants to hang on to it, because it's a very distinctive place to be in. You're set apart. But I made this decision, it seems only recently, not to be set apart. I would like to be healed now.

I am beginning to act in my own behalf, doing things I wouldn't have done a year ago, like taking a class that I'd always wanted to take. Not too long ago, I wrote to the surgeon who operated on Don. I told him how awful the experience was for me. I said that if he had just come to me, taken my hand or looked into my eyes, somehow connected with me, it would have eased the moment. It would have made it more human. I didn't get an answer, but I felt better having written.

In hindsight, I believe now that if you don't have emotional support, it behooves you to look for someone. If you don't have a Center, I think you have to ask. You have to ask your church, synagogue or neighbors, or look in the Yellow Pages under "self-help."

I feel a straight path inside me now that is open and moving forward. The road is very long, so it doesn't matter if I go ten miles today or half a mile. For a long time, I've been doing the mechanical acts of life but feeling dead. Maybe that's the normal process, like putting yourself under the snow until spring. I've been on "stop" and now I'm saying "go."

PROFESSIONAL SUPPORT

Although experiences like Holly's are all too common, there are many doctors and nurses who are in tune with emotional needs. In the main, however, those who are committed primarily to saving lives cannot be expected to provide a major part of one's support network.

Grief counseling has become a specialty, and now there are professional caregivers who have reexamined their own beliefs about death and who can offer an excellent interim solution for people who are experiencing special problems in healing from loss. While those who lose a loved one are bound to miss that special person throughout their lives, particularly at certain nostalgic moments, chronic grief requires attention.

Bereavement specialist Dr. Robert Stevenson suggests: "It is a useful analogy to think of grief as a medicine. When taken in the proper amount, it will heal." What's the proper amount? An old folk saying warned that to grieve longer than a year and a day is unkind to the dead, because it prevents them from resting in peace. Of course, such an arbitrary time span doesn't take the individual nature of the grieving experience into consideration. If we were able to write an Rx for loss, it would read: "Take as needed: the time to listen to your feelings and experience them. Continue to honor your struggle." This prescription works best when self-administered in the company of supportive people.

Counseling may be in order if you persistently feel:
• Isolated and unable to relate to other people

57

- Fearful or panicky
- Guilty, hostile or resentful
- Unable to resume normal activities
- Helpless and depressed
- Physically distressed

Professional and/or self-help support can ease us over the rough spots and often accelerate recovery. No one, however, can set our schedule for us. We have our own inner seasons, and like flowers we bloom in our own time.

6

Who Shall Grieve?

Don't judge any man until you have walked two moons in his moccassins.
                              —native American proverb

One summer afternoon, a woman came walking up the Center driveway carrying a small package. She was beaming.

"This is a thank you," she said, holding out some Saran-wrapped cheese and crackers. "I was lost, and you found me."

It turned out that she had just come over from Germany and a few days earlier had gotten lost in the neighborhood. Seeing the words Center for Help in Time of Loss on our front lawn, she'd stopped to ask directions from John, the young man who happened to be mowing the grass at the time. He'd pointed her toward her destination, and now she was back to thank him for his help. We started to explain what sort of loss the Center handles, but since she had little understanding of English and was so delighted with John's help, we didn't belabor the point.

The truth is, loss is such a universal experience

that it almost defies categorization. Generally, people come to the Center after the death of a loved one or because they're facing a life-threatening illness of their own or of a family member. They may also come because of a divorce or separation. Although we limit our volunteer at-home support to patients with progressive rather than chronic illness, the Center's ultimate purpose is to ease the stress and isolation that are common to losses of all kinds. While we recognize special problems that are unique to certain losses, we try to identify with feelings rather than compare differences. A reluctance to lay comparisons aside may prolong the recovery process, keeping people separate and isolated by "specialness."

THE RIGHT TO GRIEVE

Over and over again we hear people at the Center say, "I have no right to be so upset when I see what other people are going through," almost as if grief operated on a merit system. Our society seems to make value judgments about whose loss justifies grief and whose doesn't. The fact is, what we value most will cause us the greatest grief when we lose it, and this is based on a personal determination that no one else can make for us.

At the Center we believe simply that if you're suffering from a loss, no matter what its nature, you are in grief and value judgments are irrelevant. Actually, such judgments only add to people's stress, forcing them to repress what they feel or to feel guilty because they're in pain or, in some cases, because they aren't. Unfortunately, none of us is immune to the sanctions of the world, and when our pain is judged unworthy, we are affected. A divorcée whose husband had remarried, for instance, was shaken by his death. Overhearing comments like "What's she so upset about, they've been apart for ten years" made her feel guilty and angry and added to her sense of isolation.

Another divorced woman recalled her rage when a widow told her: "You wouldn't know how terrible it is to lose a husband after forty wonderful years. After all, your marriage was so unhappy." In many cases, the death of a marriage is experienced as a great loss by both spouses. People often mourn deeply for "what might have been." This may hold true for any unresolved or difficult relationship. "I was shocked at my own reaction to my mother's death," a woman in her early forties confided. "She'd been a real terror in my life ever since I was little, but I felt so sorry for her at the end. Now that she couldn't hurt me anymore, I could see for the first time how little happiness she'd had in her life. She looked so lost and childlike before she died." The daughter feared that her friends, who had heard her complain so bitterly about her mother, would accuse her of being a hypocrite if she showed anything but relief after the death.

When we do not sanction grief in ourselves or others, we are robbed of our experience and left with no space in which the healing can occur. What happens, for instance, to the person whose married lover dies? Society may not have approved of the relationship, but the impact is there.

At the Center's support groups, the moderator will suggest that participants try not to look at their own loss in comparison with those of other people and that they let no one rob them of their grief. To emphasize the commonality of loss, the moderator may even choose a special reading. The poem that follows, written by a staff member, is an example.

A county fair, perhaps,
In a booth where homemade preserves usually are,
We lay our pain upon a table. I bring mine in a Mason jar.

"This one looks empty." The judge unscrews the top and
A thin gray vapor drifts out. He sputters, "Make it stop."
"How do you get rid of this?" He points to the door.
"I don't know," I answer, "I never opened the lid before."

Before I go, I want to know what you put on the table.
Removed from its jar, without its label, show me your pain.
Is it a wild thing with frantic wings or
A chunk of uncut stone?
Solid, or is it hollow?
Let me touch it.
Is it so unlike my own?

INVISIBLE WOUNDS

In some cases, loss may not be recognized at all. The grief of young siblings, for example, is often overlooked. Small children who have recently lost a brother or sister may simply be told "Go out and play now" and be expected to behave as though nothing had happened. Young people in general are not encouraged to grieve. Left to their own devices, adolescents rarely seem to discuss feelings of loss with their peers. When the loss goes unresolved, the result may be that they develop problems with alcohol, drugs or some other form of destructive behavior. Jenny, for example, a teenager who came to support group when five family members died in a plane crash, told us: "I used to feel as if I were in a glass isolation booth, but since group I can say how I feel. I've even learned to listen, too."

Fathers who lose a child are often neglected as well. Most of the attention is generally focused on the grieving mother, and since men are often expected to be "stoic" anyway, they aren't quick to reach out for help. The picture seems to be changing, since more men have recently been making use of support groups. But they still come to the Center in fewer numbers than women do and often only with the purpose of helping others rather than themselves.

That was the reason Scott gave for contacting us. Actually, it was no small miracle that he was willing to reach out at all. Scott's wife had been through a long bout with cancer, and he had taken over her care as well as that of their four children. Eventually, he wound up with no driver's license because his insurance ran out, and no way of making a living. "Most of the time I didn't even know where we'd be sleeping at night," he told us. "My children were small, and they needed a father and a mother, but my wife was so ill that I had to be both.

"I tried all the agencies, but they weren't fast enough. I turned bitter when I didn't get help. What I minded most of all was pouring my heart out for nothing. I don't usually ask for things, but this was for the kids. They were little soldiers, and if it hadn't been for them I doubt I would have tried so hard. Toward the end, we were in a motel—six of us in one room. I was sure they would throw us out. I went everywhere, even to the Salvation Army. It felt like the bombs were going off, and yet it seemed that the very people I called for help were detonating the bombs. They'd say, 'We can't do anything now, we'll send out a representative to assess.'

"When my wife finally died in the hospital, I didn't know how to tell the children, but when I got home I didn't have to explain—they knew by the look on my face.

"Last spring we moved into a house. It isn't exactly what I want, but compared to a motel, or sleeping in the car with a sick wife and four kids in the back seat, it's fine. As soon as we got settled, I went to work for a chemical company until I got hurt on the job. But there was a blessing in that, because I had a chance to work on my poetry and had two poems published. That gave me confidence at a time when I really needed it—when I had nothing else left.

65

"Maybe I'm becoming more like my father. I always liked his style. You could tell him the world was falling apart, and he would go on with a little song. I miss my parents a lot since they died. I often think about the days when they were deacon and deaconess in the Baptist church, and the long hours I had to sit on those hard benches. I remember my mother telling me once, 'You know, you're going to need God before He needs you.' When reality struck, I was sorry I couldn't tell her, face to face, 'You were right.' Growing up, I had friends, but in high school I was the only black person in my class and I was wary of ethnic jokes, so I started keeping my distance. Now I do socialize with God. I'm beginning to gravitate toward people a little more.

"When I saw the ad from the Center asking for volunteers, I thought maybe people are going through experiences like mine and I could give hope. I took the volunteer training course and utilized one of the support groups for myself. I still find it hard to open up to people, though. It's easier to put my feelings on paper."

The following is one of Scott's poems that he wanted to share.

FOR YOU?

If your heart or mind has never felt sorrowed,
If ill winds of life have allowed you to pass,
If you've never felt saddened by another's misfortunes,
Read not these words.
They're for the green, in dark grass.

If you've never felt shattered by life's crushing moments
Read not these words.
They are not meant for you.

ANTIDOTE TO ISOLATION

Scott's experience illustrates the most pervasive symptom of loss: a sense of being separated, not only from what has been lost but feeling different and cut off from everyone else. This sense of isolation isn't always of our own making. Unlike national catastrophes, which draw people together for strength, personal tragedies may go almost unrecognized. A shared disaster like the shuttle failure or the death of a celebrity such as John Lennon allows people to drain off some of their anxiety about immortality. But when the loss is next door, it may be too close for comfort and people are apt to look the other way.

We may also keep our grief to ourselves because we feel that no one else would be able to identify with our own personal, unique experiences. Vinnie, for example, had buried the frightening facts of his childhood for so long that it was only after four years of therapy that he himself became aware of them. As a young boy, he had been brutally abused and assaulted by various family members. As he began to unlock his memories, there came a point when he needed confirmation that he was not totally alone and that perhaps other people had experienced similar traumas.

"Even though I began to acknowledge what had happened to me," he says, "I needed to connect, to reach out and affirm my being with other people. The total cover-up within my family had meant a denial of my whole experience. I operated mostly through my intellect rather than my feelings, and I related to other people by doing things for them, because I had no idea what it was just to love or be loved for no good reason.

"I was in my early thirties by the time those totally repressed memories began to surface. I think my ability to deny what had happened to me as a child was what allowed me to keep my sanity up to that point, and until therapy I lived a very isolated and circumscribed life. It was quite by accident that I found the Center. As I began to confront my past, I decided to start a self-help group for people like myself who had been battered

67

when they were children and who now had problems in relationships. Someone put me in touch with Mary so that I could find out how to go about it. She offered me the opportunity to set up my own group at the Center. That was around May of 1980, and I gave myself until May of 1981 to see if a group was feasible.

"I started by attending the Center's general support group for my own healing. In addition to my therapy, group was a very powerful tool. And by coincidence, I found someone else there who had been a battered child. It was like finding a long-lost brother. Slowly I began to realize that no matter what tragedy anybody had been through, the feelings were the same. The fact that I was a physically and emotionally battered person provoked feelings that are not so different from the feelings of a person dying of cancer or the feelings of someone who has lost a husband. The rage, the depression, the sense of being a victim are all there.

"Most of us have been taught that unless we stand on our own two feet and handle everything, we're not worthy people. When you first realize there are things in life that you can't handle by yourself, you feel guilty. To picture yourself as a tower of strength and to try to live up to that image is really more destructive than what you're going through. Besides that, I kept asking myself what was wrong with me. What kind of terrible person was I, that this had happened to me?

"When I found someone else who had been battered, I felt much less guilty and isolated. And when all the other people in group kept expressing feelings similar to mine, I began to see that I wasn't so different. This gave me permission to say things I'd never dared say to myself before. As I watched other people get better and put their lives together, I was encouraged.

"I wanted to put back what I'd received, so I went

on speaking engagements, stuffed envelopes, worked as a volunteer with terminal patients and helped train other volunteers. Helping others helped me to go beyond my early experiences. Eventually, I found a willingness in myself to forgive the past. Now I'm able to share my recovery as well as my pain."

WHICH WAY TO THE MAINSTREAM?

Vinnie's story illustrates the universal quality of loss, and his experience at the Center points out the benefits of being in a general support group for losses of all kinds. On the other hand, we have found that specialty groups serve a function, too. At the Center we have two parents' groups: one for parents who have lost children to AIDS, the other for child loss of any kind. These groups help people identify specific problems immediately, but all parents are encouraged to enter the weekly support group for general loss when they feel they're ready.

Grieving children and adolescents who come to the Center are grouped by age, and special methods such as play and art therapy are used to unlock feelings. The losses in these groups vary in nature.

Our widow/widower group meets only for lectures and workshops, and members are expected to work through the grieving process in the general support group. We have found that going from a special to a general group helps them gain a new perspective and fosters a sense of forward movement, helping them to enter the mainstream of life more gently.

Our cancer survivor group, burn survivor group and nurses' support group operate on yet another model, using discussion and special topics as part of the format. Since we believe that joining is healing, all these groups serve as a means and an end in themselves.

But what happens when there is no group for a special need? One of the main functions of the Center is to act as a connector to resources in the community. If we're unable to offer direct support, we can usually find what is required. For example, when the AIDS crisis prompted us to seek appropriate resources, an answer came in the form of the New Jersey Buddies—a group that provides volunteer home support for AIDS patients and their families. One of the original Buddy members, Bob Sproul, believes that volunteer training is an essential part of his program and has asked the Center to help train these volunteers.

In our role as a connector, we've also put people in touch with one another by phone when they're unable to come to support group. An understanding friend at the other end of the line can be as helpful in cutting through isolation as meeting in person. That's how it is for Mary and Selma, who have never even seen each other. Both women have multiple sclerosis, and both are confined to wheelchairs. They probably wouldn't have met under ordinary circumstances because they come from very different backgrounds. Their initial experiences with multiple sclerosis had been somewhat different, too. Selma's condition began right after her second child was born:

"I put on a pair of high heels, and I couldn't walk in them too well. I didn't give it much thought until quite a while later when I got up from a nap, cramped and unable to walk on my right foot. I developed a limp that came and went, but the doctors couldn't find anything. They just gave me tranquilizers for my nerves. All the pills did was make me depressed. Somehow I managed to get along until our next child was born. By then I was tired, I was limping, and I couldn't control my right arm. When I went into the hospital for tests, I had to sign my name and I just happened to glance down at the chart. That's when I saw the letters: MS. That was thirty years ago, and in those days they didn't tell you much. Maybe I didn't want to know too much, either. I remember, that same day, the nurse coming into my room and telling me I had some sort of condition but it wasn't serious. I just looked at her and said, 'Maybe if I were standing where you are, I'd say the same thing, but I have three little ones at home.'

"By the time our youngest child was through high school, I finally had to admit that I wasn't doing too well. I had no mother or father to help out, and I'd been determined to raise the children, so I'd managed, but now I couldn't keep going the same way and eventually I went into the wheelchair.

"I do pretty well when I'm alone, but people make me nervous—that is, except my family, who have been wonderful. Herbert, my husband, is my support and my best friend. I'm not in any pain, but I have my bad days. There's no medicine yet for what I have, but there is something that gives me a boost every day—that's a phone call from Mary."

These calls are just as important to Mary:

"Selma's the only one I can talk to who knows just what I'm going through, although our stories aren't exactly the same. I was always a very athletic person, and then suddenly, in the spring of 1955, my legs started bothering me. I went to our family doctor, who diagnosed me the first visit. We had good talks. He'd say to me, 'Mary, don't ever give in to fear.' I stopped working at the end of that year and stayed home because I didn't feel too well. Then, much to my surprise, I found out I was pregnant. I had the most wonderful nine months—and even better, Johnny came into my life, all eight pounds and nine ounces of him.

"My husband always seemed to have difficulty coping with my illness, and finally, by the time Johnny

71

was sixteen, we separated. I found out that I could be independent, that I had a lot of friends I didn't know I had. I found out that people liked me for myself. I never had trouble talking about the fact that I had multiple sclerosis. When I began using the wheelchair in 1979, I had to rely more on myself and God. I could pretty well accept what was happening in my life, but when it came to something like my high school reunion, I didn't want any of my classmates to see me confined to a chair, so I didn't go.

"Selma and I started talking on the phone—briefly at first, until we heard about a mutual friend's son who was near death. In our concern for the family, we grew closer. Although we've never met face to face, we're really very close friends now. We have good times talking on the phone, and we laugh. Selma seems like such a lady to me. Sometimes I swear a bit, and tell a few nasty jokes. At least I've gotten her to say 'damn' once in a while."

Selma says she couldn't possibly meet Mary now: "She thinks I'm such a lady! If she ever met me, I know she'd be disappointed. Besides, it's easier to talk to Mary because we've never met. It's as if there were a kind of screen between us, so we can say anything we want. Most of all, there's laughter."

"I know Selma would be very disappointed if she ever met me," Mary says. "Her wardrobe is much more coordinated than mine. As a matter of fact, we even got into shopping together. Selma got me started in this home-shopping club on cable TV. I started buying and buying. I purchased all my Christmas presents that way, and Selma got all her Hanukkah shopping done. We've learned a lot from each other. Selma and I have a kind of joke now: when anything important comes up, one of us will call the other and say, 'I have something to tell you. Are you sitting down?'

"You don't need to talk face to face to have that kind of freedom. I think that only comes when people identify with each other—that's when they begin talking heart to heart."

7

Holidays and Hope

The holiest of all holidays
are those kept by ourselves in
silence and apart: the secret anniversaries
of the heart.

—Henry Wadsworth Longfellow

$\mathcal{J}$n the first year after a loss, hardly a day goes by without some reminder of how life used to be. The first snowfall, the first crocus or the first day of school stirs memories that make us even more conscious than usual that something is gone from our lives. What used to be a personal red-letter day—an anniversary, a birthday—becomes a time of private sorrow. And the public holidays thrust us into situations that force us to decide how we're going to live in the world. The most difficult time of all comes when everyone else is celebrating the season of joy and we are in our season of grief.

Thanksgiving, Christmas and the New Year can loom like insurmountable obstacles on the road ahead. Social worker Lois Lorenz, the Center's director of training and education, has helped many grieving people to cope with the stress of holidays during her ten years with Hospice and at the American Cancer Society. "What I emphasize," Lois says, "is taking a bit more charge of these times instead of simply allowing them to happen and becoming a victim to whatever comes up." Lois suggests that people think through what is going to be the most difficult for them. Then they can try to build in some mechanisms that can ease these situations. She says, "I think one of the clearest examples was a man I worked with last year. His wife had died in August, leaving him with three small children, and the upcoming holidays made him apprehensive. He just didn't know how to handle them. He and his wife had made it a tradition to decorate the tree with ornaments collected from various trips. Each ornament had a significance of its own. What he finally decided to do was sit down with the ornaments three weeks before Christmas and go over them one by one to rehearse what he was going to feel. He knew the children would be upset enough as it was, and he didn't want an unexpected outburst on his part to distress them even further. He said that sorting through the ornaments was an ordeal, but it was better than letting out those raw emotions in front of the children."

Lois also suggests that on a holiday visit, warning friends beforehand can take some of the awkwardness out of the moment when you have to leave the room and be alone for a while. She tries to run through the coming holidays as concretely as possible: what you might expect to come up against and what you can build in to make it a little easier on yourself.

Many people opt to establish new holiday patterns right away. A few, like Mary Ann, choose to confront the pain head-on.

Mary Ann's Story

Only a month after my husband's death, I was on my way to Bermuda, taking the trip we had planned as our thirtieth anniversary celebration. I didn't know if I could

78

handle going alone, but I could give it a try. And if I couldn't stand it, I could always come home.

I can remember sitting on the reefs in Bermuda, watching the water come up and thinking that somebody else in my place might be sitting there contemplating suicide. But I didn't want to die. I felt there still had to be something wonderful left for me to experience. I also remember being in an elevator with a honeymoon couple and thinking I could melt into pieces and cry my heart out. But instead I just thought, I've stood where they're standing and one day they'll have to stand where I am. That consoled me—that I did have that share of happiness.

I was fifteen when I met Nick. We both came from the same parish and our lives centered around the church. We were married a few months after my nineteenth birthday. We were very blessed in that we were always called together in our commitments. Of course, sometimes he did things just with the men, like the Athletic Association events, but if there was a fund-raiser I was right by his side, working with him. Our call always came together and when we didn't hear the call, we didn't hear it together.

That first year alone convinced me of something I'd learned almost fifteen years before Nick died. We were on a weekend retreat when I heard something that changed my whole outlook: "Know yourself, accept yourself, and be yourself." I'd begun to make these ideas part of my life. Nick's death has only added to that deep mental and spiritual growth. I know I'm a "me" who exists and who is worthwhile no matter what happens.

Almost from the moment of loss, there was all this dreadful pain, but by the same token there was all this wonderful joy and hope for life, and both were real and happening at the same time. I don't believe God takes

79

away the pain, but rather He gives me the grace to work through it as courageously as I can. Part of that grace is the other people He puts in my life to encourage me. Encouragement doesn't mean saying, "C'mon, you've got to get on with your life." That's not allowing you to be who you are at that time and place in your grief. People encourage me by acknowledging me as a person in my own right. They encourage me by smiling at me when I accomplish something or when I'm just being me. In the midst of grief, I discovered that I have a sense of humor, too. People tell me that they'd seen glimpses of my humor in the past, but that it was never brought out before. My husband was always the funny one; I was always the straight guy. I think I've let my humor surface to show people that my deep faith doesn't mean that I'm some "holier than thou" person. I'm well aware of just how human I am. Believing in God doesn't fill the emptiness. He doesn't sit down and have a cup of coffee with me or hold my hand.

In the beginning, the dinner hour was the most difficult, especially for someone who likes to cook and fuss like I do. I loved being there for my husband, and suddenly he wasn't there for me to fuss over. On my first Valentine's Day alone, I made a candlelight dinner for one. I sat down to a glass of wine and a full course dinner. I did it for myself.

Not long after that dinner, I went to the Center for the first time. That night, I wasn't feeling out of control or in much pain. I got there early, and while I was helping the moderator set up chairs, I told her about how I'd gone to Bermuda alone and how I'd just come back from a trip to the Holy Land. She seemed to be in awe, telling me how terrific she thought I was. Then I went into group. As soon as I started to talk, I tell you the pain was just awful. I started sobbing, choking on my tears. I couldn't even get a word out, I was crying so hard. I spent the next year at group doing my grief work.

A few weeks after I started at the Center, a friend called me to ask what I was going to do about work. She told me I'd make a wonderful receptionist, but that God was not going to call me on the phone with a job offer and that I'd better go out and look for one. But the telephone *did* ring. On March 14, the day before my fiftieth birthday, a widow whose husband had been friendly with Nick told me that there was an opening for a temporary job where she worked and asked if I was interested. On that following Monday, March 19, which is, by the way, the feast day of St. Joseph the Worker, I went to work for the first time in twenty-eight years. I got up each morning, washed my face and hands, combed my hair, put on my make up and went out to meet life. I still had to come home and face the loneliness, and I had to face me. No matter how busy you are or how many people you fill your day with, there's always that moment when you have to be alone with yourself.

But I did begin to develop a real confidence—an assurance that in some way I was still needed here, and that I had a function to fill. My temporary job turned into a permanent one, but I'd begun to feel that I had more to offer than what this clerical job demanded of me. So I marched myself in to see the head of personnel, and asked if there were any secretarial positions open. She wanted to know how many words a minute I could type, and when I told her forty, she just shrugged and said if I wanted to take the test that was fine, but forty words wasn't good enough to be a secretary.

I don't know how anyone else would explain what happened, but when the buzzer signaled that the test was over, my score was sixty-five words per minute with only three mistakes. There's no way I could have done that on my own, so I have to believe it's a blessing that I'm a secretary now.

My feeling of confidence has spilled into many areas of my life. At support group, I began to realize that the way I was willing to share, and what I said there, was having an effect on other people, so I wasn't surprised when I was asked to become a group moderator. What I've learned from the group is that nobody has to have the answers for anyone else. We don't solve other people's problems, because they have the solutions lying right within themselves.

I know that I'll always miss Nick, and that whatever good is happening for me must make him proud and happy. I've been given much to sustain me, and I want to share that with other people. I had a young widow come up to me at group and tell me that I was an inspiration to her because of the colors I wear, and my make up, and the way my hair is always fixed just so. She told me that the morning after we first met, she put on make up for the first time since her husband died. A week later, she came up to me all excited: "You won't believe it," she said, "but somebody just told me what an inspiration I was to her."

It passes on—and that's what hope is.

SUPPORTING EVERY STAGE

The best encouragement we can get is to watch as someone who sat where we sit moves on and gains strength. And sometimes, even when people are facing death themselves, the support of others who are going through similar experiences can enrich their days.

Steven was looking for that kind of support when he came to the Center. "I can't talk to too many people," he said. "I don't want to tell them all the details or have to reassure them that everything's going to be just fine." Steven's prognosis was not hopeful. His cancer was highly metastasized. "I've made it clear to everyone that I don't want to hear biblical or religious stuff," he said. "Going to a clergyman isn't what I want. I prefer to talk to people who know what I'm going through and who don't feel like they have to foist any opinions on me."

The thing that bothered Steven most was the breakdown of his relationship with friends. "We've had acquaintances really go out of their way for us," he explained, "but some of our good friends just can't handle it." One of his best friends, visiting him after his first surgery, stayed a few minutes before whispering, "Steve, I just can't deal with what you have," and then walked out. That was the last time they ever saw each other.

Steven's wife and children used the support groups, and he himself took the Center's volunteer training course so that he could help others learn what he felt patients really need. In turn, a young woman at the Center taught Steven's wife macrobiotic cooking for the diet he was on. Steven outlived the doctor's predictions and found people he could share openly with until his death in the spring of 1986.

Though our purpose is to ease the stress of loss, we at the Center have many chances to celebrate new life, too. Seanlean, for instance, who came for help when she was seven months pregnant, had been diagnosed with Hodgkin's disease but did not know the stage of her illness because her doctors wanted to hold off further testing until the baby was born. Having grown up in an orphanage, Seanlean feared most of all that her baby might have to grow up in the same way. On her own and working since her early teens, she was unmarried and had been looking forward to the new baby as being the first real family she'd ever known. Now she had to endure the two-month waiting period until a true diagnosis could be made.

From the moment she joined the cancer survivors' support group, Seanlean found a surrogate family. Most hopeful of all was the presence of a young mother in the group who had survived cancer, and the two women became fast friends. And then, just before Thanksgiving, Jade Lin, a healthy baby girl, was born. Two weeks later, Seanlean had more to be thankful for—she was diagnosed as having "first-stage Hodgkin's," and her illness was curable.

Any time people come together and see each other's interests being similar to their own, it's a special occasion. The celebrants can best be described by these words of psychiatrist Eric Fromm: ". . . those whose hope is strong see and cherish all signs of new life, and are ready at every moment to help the birth of that which is ready to be born."

8

Who Am I?

Perhaps today, perhaps tomorrow,
You will look into this glass,
And understand the sinless light you see belongs to you.
The loveliness you look on is your own.
                                        —A Course in Miracles

No other subject seems to command as much attention as self-image. Who we are seems to be most clearly defined by how much of ourselves we invest in our "special relationships." When we lose someone who has become part of our identity, we seem to lose a part of ourselves. From her experience in counseling those in grief, Lois Lorenz has concluded: "Not only do you suffer the blow of losing a significant part of your self-image, but now you have to become almost a new person." According to Lois, many people fight this change because it's an extremely difficult one, but those people who have the courage to change will usually grow in ways they never thought they'd be capable of. "It's not just leaving behind the person you've lost," she says. "It's leaving behind a large part of yourself as well."

Not knowing who you are is more than a little uncomfortable, and redefining the self after a loss can be a central issue of the grieving process. This was certainly the case for Emily, who slowly discovered parts of herself she never knew existed.

Emily's Story

Until recently, I'd forgotten all about the butterflies. What a surprise to find ourselves in the migration path of the monarchs! It was August of 1982, and I was vacationing at Long Beach Island in New Jersey with my sons, Raymond and Greg, who were twelve and fourteen at the time. Eric, the man I expected to marry had come with us. I remember how peaceful it was. Every evening I'd sit on the porch of our beach house and watch the sun go down behind the large cross on the monastery opposite us while the black-and-orange butterflies swarmed and perched all around. I felt there was something significant about the brown-robed monks, the setting sun and the butterflies, but I had no idea what sort of transformation was about to take place in all of our lives.

On the Saturday night after we got home, Raymond and Greg decided to camp out in our backyard with another friend. At three o'clock in the morning, I was awakened by a banging on the door. The converted chicken coop that served as a tent was on fire. Raymond was in shock from severe burns, and Greg was nowhere to be found. Their friend T.R. had managed to drag Raymond, in flames, out of the coop and had rolled him on the ground to extinguish the fire. The trucks and emergency vehicles arrived soon after. We didn't learn until later that the boys had fallen asleep with a candle still lit and it had fallen into Raymond's sleeping bag.

I must have been numb sitting in the waiting room of the burn unit at Westchester Medical Center. Raymond was critical, with third-degree burns over 65 percent of his body. Greg was still missing. I didn't know that he had wandered into the house late that morning, still in shock but not badly hurt. The doctors held out little hope for Raymond's survival.

None of us wanted to stay at the house where it happened, so for the next week we camped out in the Center: my daughter Karen and her fiancé, Greg and Eric and I. My ex-husband Earle was there a lot, too. We all needed each other. I had known Mary several years before she started the Center, and I was one of the founding members. I don't believe anyone is ever really prepared for a trauma when it happens, but I felt surrounded by love and this eased the situation. Everybody pitched in. A woman whose husband was dying of cancer even sent over meals she had cooked for us.

The next few months were touch and go until it became evident that Raymond was going to make it. A fire can do terrible things. But Raymond survived the burns that covered him from the waist up. He was learning to feed himself after losing all the fingers on his left hand and the tips of his fingers on the right one. Week after week, he went into the operating room and back to his bed to become strong enough for the next surgery.

I never had a sense of helplessness, because I felt that I was there to console him and love him. And when he finally came home, I was there to do everything for him: to be his hands, to do the bandage changes that were excruciating for him and to comfort him afterwards and to perform the endless back-scratching that unfortunately never seemed to relieve the maddening itch of new skin and healing nerve endings. I had a function. I was his mother, and I was fulfilling that role. It didn't leave much time for anything else.

I think on an unconscious level I must have known that something was wrong, because one night I said to Eric, "Sometimes I get the feeling that you don't want to be here." He nodded and said that sometimes he did feel that way, but he couldn't just leave me in the middle of this. I remember saying something that would come back to haunt me for a long time: "I'm not alone," I told him with great confidence. "God is with me." I honestly felt that way at the time. I felt I had a direct connection and that I would be sustained no matter what.

Raymond had been home for about six months when those words began to sound hollow to me. It was a hot June day, and Eric and I were driving home after looking for a new place to live.

"I've been thinking about that conversation we had," he said, "and I feel I should leave."

It was like a having a wet towel snapped in my face. I couldn't speak. There were so many feelings that I couldn't separate them. Rage and fear and something very old and familiar—a sense of abandonment that had lurked somewhere inside me all my life. At that moment I felt that God, too, had walked out the door.

I don't think I realized until then how dependent I was on that special relationship. The same sense of abandonment had been there during my divorce, but I was convinced that I'd worked through those feelings. Later, when my friendship with Eric turned into a meaningful relationship, I remember thinking: At last, here's the man I always wanted—someone stable, consistent, who will love me unconditionally. We had a real heart connection, and I was certain it would last forever. Now it was gone.

The next two years were very painful ones. Raymond was doing well, but he had a lot of surgery ahead and we were constantly traveling to the Shriners Burn Institute in Boston. Greg moved in with his father, who could give him the loving attention he needed. People were supportive, but I think most of them surmised that I needed help because of Raymond's circumstances and not because I'd lost Eric. I was still a mother but I was no longer one half of a couple. A friend of mine who is a counselor helped ease some of the confusion when I asked her why so many families fall apart after a crisis. She explained that when two people are very needy, they're unable to nurture one another so they often require outside help until they can be there for each other.

Only recently, I had an insight while I was driving home from work. I remembered all the nurturing Eric gave us while I was running back and forth to the hospital for Raymond. One night I'd come home to find dinner waiting and Eric sitting with Greg doing homework. They had eaten, and Eric had gotten my favorite baked chicken for me. I was in a bad way that evening. It was the first time I'd seen Raymond without his bandages. They had him hooked up to a t-pole so that the grafts wouldn't be disturbed. He was hung there like Christ on the cross, crucified. Coming home that night to a warm, caring place was a gift.

I wonder sometimes why Eric and I didn't seek professional help for ourselves then. We were not unaware—plenty of people had warned us that we'd better take some time for ourselves. But the whole thing just consumed us.

After the separation, I spent a lot of time at support group and being counseled. And I began to connect my feelings of abandonment to a time back in childhood. I guess I was born thinking that life is safe and changeless. I had a loving mother, father and sister, and most of all I had my great-grandmother. She was my security blanket, and I never left her side. She was an invalid in a wheelchair. My mother took care of her while she, in turn, took care of me. When I was born she said to my mother, "Give me my baby." I have this vague recollection of being about seven or eight years old and sitting in a church at her funeral, thinking I wasn't going to let anyone see me cry. The next thing I remember is being eleven or twelve and not having any feelings about her one way or the other. And then one day at the Center, when Charles Lochner was playing some of his music that helps unlock feelings, I suddenly saw my great-grandmother's face as if she were there. I saw every wrinkle, her white hair pulled back in a bun, her white apron, her blue-veined hands. When I mentioned this to Gregg Furth, who was counseling at the Center, he pointed out that children can't comprehend when someone is suddenly taken away by death.

I went back to taking care of terminal patients, which I'd been doing before Raymond's accident, with a deeper understanding that all of us were seeking the same things together—a way to let go and accept. Two more years passed before the emotional healing was evident. I went through all the phases—the shattering, the asking for help, a feeble hope that I would feel better someday, and the honesty to look within. I'm still working on patience. It was something Charlie said that helped my shift in perspective. He talked about life being a process, not a race to win, and that you could own that struggle and honor it in yourself and other people. That allowed me to ease up on myself—and recognize that wherever I was in my healing was fine for the moment. And slowly I did begin to sense something inside of me that felt very stable and very consistent—the very attributes I had once looked for outside myself. I realized then that I had always tried to give my power to others. Now I would have to own that as well. The little girl crying for her great-grandmother is still there, but I don't have to let her run my life, and I can comfort that part of myself. I don't really see myself as a victim anymore.

Greg is back home now, and Raymond just got his

driver's license. They double-date with their special girl friends. My relationships are much different than they used to be—less dependent, more empowering. The house rocks with music, because Raymond is usually rehearsing with his band. Even without any fingers on his left hand, he's an incredible drummer.

One evening not long ago, I was rereading a book called *Illusions*. Lori, a young woman whom I took care of until she died, used to quote from the book all the time. I remember her reading a passage aloud about two friends knowing each other better in the first moment they meet than acquaintances know each other in a thousand years. I think of her often. As I skimmed through the book, a phrase caught my eye and suddenly I was back on the porch of that summer house, watching the monks and the monarchs in the rays of the setting sun, and I knew what it meant when I read: "What the caterpillar calls the end of life, the Master calls a butterfly."

THE GRIEVING FAMILY

Just as an individual must redefine the self after a death, the family unit, too, undergoes a similar change. The impact on the family might be compared to a shipwreck with the survivors left temporarily adrift in a life raft. In the immediate aftermath, the individuals are apt to cling together for safety, but in time each one must find his or her own inner balance. The trip can be quite rocky until the raft reaches shore. If a family has underlying problems to begin with, a loss tends to magnify those difficulties. Even the family with firm bonds will have to reorganize in some ways, because its form has been changed. Since no two people seem to grieve in exactly the same way, the differences among family members need to be honored. Not only compassion for one another, but being gentle with oneself, is generally more conducive to unity than assuming the role of the stoic to protect one's spouse or children.

Despite the statistics indicating that many families are unable to weather a loss, there are many that do survive and become even stronger.

All families tend to have their own myths which are handed down in some form from generation to generation. A crisis forces people to explore these myths and to decide what changes may be necessary. The courage to ask for help and the honesty to look within can be as useful to the family as a whole as to its individual members, but often each person may need to seek some special kind of support. That seemed to be the most helpful solution for a family who came to the Center after the death of a little boy.

Brian was almost nine when he was struck by a car as he rode to school on his bicycle. He received severe head injuries and was brain-dead but kept "alive" for six days until his liver could be used for a transplant to save the life of another child.

Brian left behind many memories for his father Jim, his mother Karel, and his older brother and best friend, Alex. They remember Brian's high-spirited energy and the way he gave his all no matter what he did. At Brian's funeral, instead of the usual formal flower arrangement, the family chose sprays of wildflowers: as twelve-year-old Alex put it, "Brian should have dandelions because he was a lion and wildflowers because he was wild." The organ music that filled the church was Brian's favorite—the theme from *Star Wars.*

When the initial shock of a trauma wears off, the pain sets in. The death of a child strains our belief systems and leaves a disproportionately large gap in a family. The emptiness is often temporarily filled not only with sorrow, but with anger, fear and guilt. The attempts to put things back exactly as they were are mostly futile, but hope is always present when each member of the family is willing to bring his or her own struggle to light. In the case of Brian's family, Jim and Alex are making use of the Center's grief counseling, and Karel has been coming to support group with other parents who have lost a child.

"I realize that you can't live through others," Karel says, "that you have to be at peace with yourself first." As a child of a minister, Karel says she learned first and foremost to be of service to others, and only now is she beginning to learn how to nurture herself. "I say that people can't make you happy," she explains, "but they sure can make it a lot easier. So many good people have come forth. You can't really heal alone."

MAKING ROOM FOR A MIRACLE

A life-threatening illness and the loss of a body function are bound to affect a person's self-image. For Cindi, that change was accompanied by a miracle. "You can't believe how shy and quiet I used to be before this happened," she says. Cindi was twenty-two years old when she gave birth to twins (with two little ones at home, they made a family of six) and, during her hospital stay, had a lump removed from her forearm. It turned out to be malignant. Even more devastating, she was advised that her arm would have to be amputated—that otherwise she'd be dead within two years.

"I cried hysterically," she says, "and I told my husband I didn't want to live if they had to remove my arm. He sat on the bed with me, and it was the first time I saw him cry. We cried together." Cindi resigned herself to the surgery, then underwent chemotherapy for the next eight months.

Everything was fine until three years later when an x-ray showed a lesion on Cindi's lung. There was more surgery, and more chemotherapy. Up to this point Cindi had been a person who rarely spoke up, but the hospital treatment began to get to her: "It was like a slaughter house, very clinical and insensitive." The final blow came when she was told that another operation would be necessary and that she would be called at home when a bed was available. But no call came for a month. "I was a nervous wreck," Cindi recalls, "just waiting to get it over with. I called the doctor in charge on a Sunday." The doctor was indignant that she had dared to disturb him on a weekend and told her that she would just have to wait her turn for a bed. That did it. Having had enough of being a silent victim to the disease and the impersonal treatment, Cindi called her gynecologist. He had always taken an interest in her, and now he recommended that she get her x-rays and records out of the hospital so that he could set up an appointment with a new doctor.

Oddly enough, a bed became available the very next day, but Cindi went into the hospital only to retrieve her records. By coincidence, she ran into the doctor who had given her a bad time the day before. When he asked her if she had received word about the bed, she told him off soundly. "He was with two colleagues," she says, "but that didn't stop me. After I told him what he could do with the bed, I told him that he had no right to be a doctor—that he was a fool."

From that point on, Cindi's attitude about herself seemed to change. The new doctor cared about her and never rushed her. "It made such a difference," she says. "I could believe that what he chose would be right for me." She also began to learn all she could about her disease and eventually became a kind of expert on herself.

Not that everything went smoothly after that. There was even a point when her new doctor was stymied by the continuing recurrence of the disease. One day he called her in and said he felt there was nothing more he could do. "I looked at him in surprise," she recalls, "and then I told him he would just have to come up with something. After all, I had no intention of dying." The doctor tried two different types of treatment that kept her coming and going from the hospital. The twins, about five years old by then, were completely confused by the routine, so a port was arranged at home for Cindi to administer some of the drugs herself. And still the disease continued to show up.

In 1985 Cindi was still on chemotherapy when her mother called to ask if she would like to take a trip up to St. Anne de Beauprès in Canada. "I knew she was hoping for a healing, so I agreed to go along for the weekend. I remember saying on the ride up that it would be wonderful if I never had to have chemotherapy again." Cindi's husband stayed home with the children, and Cindi and her parents spent the weekend in prayer.

"I knew when we left that something miraculous was taking place," she says. Monday morning, as she was hooked up for chemotherapy, the doctor said he had decided to stop the treatment—he wanted her to have surgery to remove whatever tumors were there. "It was like a sudden answer to my prayer that I would not have to undergo chemotherapy anymore. That surgery took place on October 24, 1985. There was a mess of tumors inside, and for precaution they implanted these radioactive iodine seeds that give off radiation for two years. Most of it is given off in the first six months, and I asked them if I was going to glow in the dark." Before Cindi left the hospital, a doctor handed her a paper stating that if she died she would have the radioactive seeds returned to the hospital. He wanted her to sign it. "Get lost," she told him. "I paid for the seeds, and I have no intention of returning them."

A few months later, Cindi asked her doctor what he thought about her prognosis. She remembers that he paused for a moment, then said quietly, "I think you'll be around to hound me for a very long time."

"I feel strongly," Cindi says, "that I have to pass on the gift I've received." She's finished the volunteer training course at the Center, and she's certain that her own experience has prepared her to help other people who may be going through the same thing. "In a way, I'm really grateful for all I've been through," she says. "If it hadn't happened, I don't know what I'd be like. I know I wouldn't be the me I am now."

9

What Am I Doing Here?

. . . at some moment I did answer Yes to Someone—or Something—and from that hour I was certain that existence is meaningful and that, therefore, my life, in self-surrender, had a goal.

—Dag Hammarskjöld

$\mathcal{J}$n an anteroom of the huge chapel at River-
side Church, where Dr. Elisabeth Kübler-Ross was
speaking on the subject of near-death experiences, a
woman approached the table we'd set up for handing
out brochures about the Center.

"Do you deal in transitions?" she asked. When it
was clear that we were puzzled by the question, she
shook her head sadly. "Death," she said. "I want to
know about death and what's on the other side."

After explaining that she was interested in contacting those who had "passed over," she added, "None
of you go far enough." Then she headed for the door,
apparently convinced that we didn't have the answers
she was looking for.

It wasn't hard to understand her need to understand. Most of us at one time or another speculate
about what we're doing here and where we're going.
Those of us who have not had a near-death experience

may find it comforting to hear reports about the "light at the end of the tunnel" and the peaceful nature of dying usually described by those who have. Still, these belong to someone else's experience, and there's a big difference between hearsay and knowing something firsthand. In the long run, most of us are left with no more than concepts about death—and these concepts are often shaken when we lose someone we love.

A PERSONAL MEANING

People who have just come to the Center are filled with "whys." Why now? Why wasn't I with him when he died? Why didn't she live long enough to see her first grandchild? And underneath is the question: Why does it always have to end this way? People have a need to make sense of what has happened to them. Rarely are there any immediate answers, and the only ones that will satisfy are those we come up with ourselves.

As people wrestle with concepts, trying to fit their experience into a framework they can accept, a subtle shift takes place. We see people at the Center gradually move out of the passive role of feeling victimized to become active participants in their own lives. They begin to seek a way to give their pain meaning, to make their suffering bear fruit. A woman who lost her seven-year-old daughter is using her musical talent to write and sing songs that offer hope and comfort. She told us that the last words her daughter Lori spoke before she died were "thank you" and she wanted to pass that on. "I started adoption proceedings almost immediately," she said. "My choice is to keep my heart open and love. Whatever gifts I have, I want to give."

Our profound need to find meaning in our lives, especially after a trauma, has been documented by psychiatrist Victor E. Frankl. Dr. Frankl first developed his theory of Logotherapy (a psychology based on

102

man's search for meaning) from his experiences as a survivor of Auschwitz and three other concentration camps. "Suffering ceases to be suffering in some way at the moment it finds a meaning," he wrote. "The striving to find a meaning in one's life is the primary motivational force in man. . . . This meaning is unique and specific in that it must and can be fulfilled by him (the individual) alone; only then does it satisfy his own will to meaning."

In line with Dr. Frankl's theory, our experience at the Center has shown that people are rarely satisfied with abstract concepts—that they generally seek and find a personal meaning that can be lived in whatever form each of them is best able to express it.

We had the opportunity to hear some people talk about their life purposes at the Center during a stress management workshop given by Matt, a volunteer, who shared his own unique search for meaning. A successful executive, Matt found his life unfulfilling until a moment of insight sent him on an intense learning journey to gurus, rabbis and Zen masters. He returned home to his family with a yearning to share his experiences with others, and when he heard about the Center, he decided to take the volunteer training course, and afterwards offered his gift of a six-session workshop to his fellow volunteers. At the first session, he asked participants to state the meaning of their lives. The responses were thoughtful and halting, because few people seemed to have put this idea into words before.

One young woman said, "I think I always wanted to be the perfect mother, but now I want . . . well, my husband would tell you I'm always trying to save the world."

Another said, "Right now I feel I'm here to honor myself, to honor other people, and to enjoy the present moments."

A man who had nursed his wife during her bout with cancer until her death said he wanted to support people who were going through similar circumstances.

A young woman said, "I think I'm here to express a certain energy. I guess I'd call it the Christ energy."

Everyone in the room had apparently chosen volunteering as a way to fulfill at least part of their special purposes.

Loss makes people aware of their need for meaning and prompts them to find a purpose that will make life worth living. Dara Lee, a member of one of our support groups, found a personal reason for going on alone at age nineteen after her mother died. She wrote this in her journal:

"It has been a long hard fight . . . and I'm glad she's out of pain. But it's really strange being a survivor. I almost feel guilty about living without her. I sat shiva with my sister and brother for only two days, instead of the customary seven, because of Rosh Hashana. It's ironic that she died near Rosh Hashana, the New Year. This truly will be a new year for me. A year alone, for the first time in my life, and I'm not too proud to admit that I'm damned scared.

"So many people I know who have dealt with death, lose their inspiration to do or achieve anything. I am the opposite way. I feel like my mom is pushing me, and expecting me to do well to make her proud. She made me realize while she was alive how important today is. Every morning you can do whatever you want, if you really want to. And if you don't do it now, you may never get the chance. As cliché as it sounds, today is the first day of the rest of my life, and I plan to go on living it to the hilt for both of us."

A SPECIAL LANGUAGE

When people confront the profoundest mystery of their

lives, and they try to fathom the meaning, symbols become more significant, because ordinary language seems too limited for such ideas. Rituals like Communion and lighting Sabbath candles allow people to express meanings that lie too deep for words. In many instances, people develop their own personal symbols that speak directly to them. A widow, for example, confided, "I think people might suspect that I'm losing my mind, but I have this special feeling about a night light that I keep in my bedroom. It has a personal connection to my husband for me, and when it's lit, I always feel his presence. I wouldn't think of traveling without it."

These special links keep a sense of communication open with those we love. They may speak to us in a dream, through a flower, the moon, a word, in a coincidence or a song. Whatever the form, the message seems to bring comfort in a language only each bereaved person can understand. Through personal symbols and rituals, our daily lives are made more profound, more sacred, more meaningful. The symbols become a way of honoring our relationships and they provide a continuity with the past.

It is not in the past or the future, however, that the search for meaning takes place. Meaning is found in the here and now. Charles Lochner, who was for many years a pastoral counselor, speaks of his own faith as having a perspective rooted in the present. "I've never looked at life as a waiting room for the next," he says. "I've always felt that this life is very important in and of itself. I believe every bit of it bears a message." Charlie believes that it is not in the extraordinary that God addresses us, but in the context of the ordinary. His view is in keeping with one of his favorite philosophers, Martin Buber, who describes it this way: ". . . what is greater for us than all the enigmatic webs at the margin

105

of being is the central actuality of an everyday hour on earth, with a streak of sunshine on a maple twig and an intimation of the eternal You."

RELATING TO THE WHOLE

No matter how unique each of us is and how different our view of the universe may be, we are related to one another and to the world. We may or may not be aware of a conscious purpose in our lives, but what we do, sometimes even the smallest acts, may have consequences we never dreamed of. The extent of our effect on other people was brought home clearly by a letter that one of our staff members showed us. Julie Dombal, a registered nurse who coordinates the Center's At Home services, told us that her father had received this letter more than thirty years ago when he was a buyer for Montgomery Ward in New York City.

It seems that a woman in Chicago had written to him asking for some wool to repair a sweater she had purchased. Julie's father, Mr. McWilliams, unable to find the appropriate wool, sent the woman a brand new sweater instead. This small, seemingly insignificant act from a stranger elicited the following response:

"Your complimentary sweater arrived yesterday. Mr. McWilliams, this letter to you is marked 'Personal' because from here on I intend to tell you how your magnanimous gesture has had an almost unbelievable effect on my new attitude.

"You see, I am a rather reticent (almost timid) person and regarded by most people as old fashioned, too square, etc. to cope with today's way of life. No windfalls have ever been mine because I can't resort to the little artful tactics and dodges that beget windfalls. Consequently, I am regarded by family and friends as a little on the hopeless side. Your gift was my big victory at long last. It made me very sure, once again, that there is nothing wrong with my outmoded code for living. Actually, you sent me much more than a red sweater. It was a full length cloak of renewed confidence.

"I want you to know some of the things I have undertaken with my reinforced self-assurance.

1. Invited my husband's employer and his wife to dinner. I have been hedging on this for six months, but I know now it will go well, and I can do a good job as hostess.

2. Began a course of automobile driving lessons—should solo sometime early next month.

3. I have tactfully advised my sister-in-law that she needn't bother to help me with plans for decorating part of our apartment. For years she has been imposing her tastes on me. I've discovered there is nothing wrong with my taste—in fact, it's rather good.

"I hope I haven't bent your ear too much. I just wanted you to know that you have done a great deal for me—more than Dale Carnegie could accomplish in six volumes. May you have all that is good all the days of your life. . . ."

PASSING IT ON

At the Center, we can't help but be aware of the effect people have on one another's lives. We see strangers come together in support group and share in each other's healing. Those who have recovered take it out into their daily lives and pass it on. Some people continue on at the Center as volunteers, working in the office, as group moderators or as speakers in the community, and visiting terminal patients at home or driving them to therapy and assisting their families.

Many health care professionals serve as volunteers. Why should a busy nurse offer to give her time? Clinical nurse specialist Mary Ann Collins explains: "It's an opportunity to practice the art of nursing rather than just the medical skills and paperwork that absorb most of us in the present health care system." There are plenty of caring nurses, Mary Ann says; in fact, there is a world of caring people. But they need a nest to land in where they can put their gifts and talents to use.

Something happens when people join together to share a common purpose. "You can't help extending yourself" is the way Joan, who balances the Center's books, puts it. "I came to do office work, but caring is just plain infectious."

Only the other day somebody brought in a news clipping on the origin of words. On the list was the word *comfort—com* meaning "together" and *fort* meaning "strength." "Together strength" is a good definition of what the Center is all about. But comfort isn't confined to a Center or a place—it's what everyone of us needs, especially in time of loss.

10

What Can I Say?

He who goes to do good must knock
At the gate.
He who goes in love finds the gate open.

—Rabindranath Tagore

$\mathcal{W}$hen someone we care about is hurting, we sit down to compose a letter or we pay a visit—and suddenly we're stymied. We get only as far as "Words cannot convey . . ." or "I'm sorry . . ."

Why is it so difficult to console? The quickest answer is that we have no language of the heart to express our deepest feelings. Even poets and writers are blocked when they try. In a collection of condolence letters by famous people, the language sounds surprisingly stilted and self-conscious. The most effective letter of the lot was written by George Bernard Shaw to a loved one whose son had been killed in the war. It says simply, "I heard the news. Damn, damn, damn, damn, damn."

But maybe it's more than the language that fails us. Dr. Jane Templeton, a psychologist who specializes in communication, believes that most of us spend our lives "longing desperately for someone to come along and break our inner code and discover who we are and at the same time desperately afraid that someone will come along and break our inner code and find out who we are."

Our inability to reach one another when it counts seems to be the high price we pay for guarding our separateness, for maintaining a discreet distance from one another. We even encourage "braving it alone" and keeping our feelings private. The public was impressed with the stoic behavior of the Kennedy family during the funeral proceedings for the President and with the report that one of their clan mottos is "Kennedys don't cry." And, more recently, a stage-and-screen celebrity described his battle against cancer as a "solitary struggle," repeating the oft quoted idea that "We're born alone and we die alone."

We at the Center might admire the courage shown in these sentiments, but we question their usefulness. In fact, these songs in praise of separateness only keep us from being in harmony with other people.

PLEASE DON'T REMIND ME

Our fear of closeness puts us in a real dilemma when we wish to offer comfort, but another fear is at work, too—and that is our fear of death. We don't like to be reminded of our vulnerability. Maybe it will happen to us someday, but for the moment it's more comfortable to dissociate ourselves from that fact of life. As a result we may dissociate from the bereaved as well. We maintain that distance, sometimes by telling ourselves that we shouldn't intrude on someone's private feelings or else by treating the grieving person as if he were not like us at all: "Nothing made me so furious as being told that I could handle my loss because I was so strong," a woman at the Center told us. "I actually had people say they were glad it was me and not them going through it because they couldn't have handled it. You'd think they were exempt from loss!"

The grieving person who is singled out for bravery may feel even worse as an object of pity. Most of us can relate to Thoreau when he wrote, "If I knew a man was coming to my house with the conscious design of doing me good, I should run for my life." Who doesn't bristle at the idea of being a charitable case? Yet, even Thoreau, a formidable loner, eventually left Walden Pond for the comforts of his fellow human beings. Whether we admit it or not, we need one another.

What all of this points up is that people who want to give comfort will somehow have to find a way around their own discomfort—and in some cases will have to plow right through it. It often takes real courage to keep our hearts open. "To love," Dr. Elisabeth Kübler-Ross wrote, "means not to impose your own powers on your fellowman, but to offer him your help. And if he refuses it, to be proud that he can do it on his own strength."

And so we go, walking on eggshells, not to do good but to bring love, not quite trusting our intentions but going all the same.

AN ETIQUETTE OF LOVE

What can we say on a condolence call?

Sometimes the best thing to say is nothing. Dr. Robert Stevenson, in his course on "Death Perspectives," tells his students that a touch or eye contact can be a lot more meaningful than dragging out the worn clichés. Because it's awkward to be silent, people grab for a phrase—and then wish they hadn't. A nurse who works with the Center confided, "I could have bitten my tongue. I wanted very much to say something helpful, so I told a friend that God must have really loved her

113

husband to take him. My friend stared at me for a moment and then said quietly, 'But we loved him, too.' "

Dr. Stevenson and his students have come up with a list of "101 Dumb Things to Say at a Funeral." High on the list are "I know just how you feel" and "It's all for the best." In fact, no one can know exactly how other people feel, and it's almost impossible to judge what's best for them.

When you first arrive for a condolence visit, Dr. Stevenson says, you don't have to say anything. Just the fact that you're there says a lot. A handshake, a hug—whatever is appropriate, as long as it's real—means more than words. Then, after you've been there awhile, you might talk about your memories of the deceased—the fun you had with him, or the last time you saw her. Talking about the person who died opens the door for those in grief to share their own memories and feelings. You're not forcing them to share, but you make it possible for them to do so without directly soliciting a response.

If you didn't know the deceased, Dr. Stevenson suggests that you talk about those qualities in the bereaved person that will serve him through grief. For example, you might point out, "I hope you can show yourself some of the kindness that you've always been willing to show others." You don't have to support the idea that sacrifice and suffering are virtues, and you can remind people in grief that it's okay to be kind to themselves.

Advice or warnings can sometimes be painful, as one widow found out when a friend leaned over at the funeral and whispered, "You think it's bad now, just wait until later when you're really alone." Although this may be true, such information is hardly helpful at the funeral.

114

All of us could probably make a long list of insensitive remarks because no one is exempt when it comes to blundering and saying the wrong thing. Charles Lochner reminds those he counsels that the world is not in grief and people often don't realize what a bereaved person may be feeling. He believes there is actually an obligation on the part of the person in grief to recognize that, no matter how foolish, the things people say are probably well-intentioned. The fact that they've come to offer comfort says they're trying.

ACTS OF KINDNESS

What we say to people in grief is much less significant than the small acts of kindness we can do for them. Dr. Stevenson urges his students not to ask what they can do for someone, but to just do it. Instead of placing the burden on the bereaved to tell you what they want and making them feel guilty for asking, he suggests that it's better to go ahead and risk doing something wrong than to do nothing at all.

A positive example of doing took place in a suburb near the Center. A mother and father who were spending most of their time in the hospital visiting their dying son came home each night to find dinner waiting for them in the refrigerator or in a slow cooker. None of the notes that accompanied the meals was ever signed. Eventually, they found out that one of the neighbors had gotten hold of a key to the house and all the people on the block were taking turns preparing meals.

"When we suffer a loss," Dr. Stevenson says, "there is a small child inside us who is hurting. And what we can do for other people is what we would do for that small child." When children are hurt, we hug them, we talk to them gently. We show them that we care and that there's still love in the world. We nurture them by preparing nice meals, by giving them emotional and physical nourishment. We don't tell them, "Grow up and act your age." We let them be where they are.

"Our society," Dr. Stevenson says, "is very good at telling people how they should feel, and it's time we cut out that nonsense." But what should we do instead? Sister Eileen McGrath, an expert in death, dying and bereavement, posed this dilemma for her listeners. "Suppose you go to your best friend's house and the door is open. You walk in to find her smashing figurines against the wall. These figurines had been brought from all over the world by her husband, who had just died. What would you do? Stop her? Walk away and pretend you hadn't seen her?" Reason says that stopping her would only block her anger, which needs to be expressed, but what about the guilt she's likely to feel later if she isn't stopped?

The incident was a real one, and Sister Eileen's solution was to go into her friend's kitchen and find some of her oldest dishes. "I ran out and started handing them to her," she said, "until she was finished smashing them."

Probably the most significant thing we can do for grieving people is to be there for them during the first year after their loss. That year is filled with anniversaries and obstacles that you can help them get through by providing the extra support they need. If you're willing to give on an open-ended basis, it's important to network with others who are willing to share in the support. It isn't practical to assume the entire role yourself, or you'll end up feeling over-burdened and resentful.

COMING FROM THE HEART

When people we care about are in pain, there may be a great temptation to try to take away their grief—to "make it all better." But we can't fix it, and our attempts might even be considered a disservice. A staff member spoke of her frustrating experience when she tried to do just that: "I wanted desperately to help a friend who had been moping for more than a year after the breakup of a relationship. I philosophized, I joked. I tried to interest her in a dozen activities. Nothing worked. Finally, I threw up my hands. 'I don't know any way to make this better,' I told her, 'but I love you, and I'm here.' My friend told me later that those words, spoken in sheer frustration, gave her one of the most comforting moments in her grief."

"I love you" and "I'm here" are the two greatest gifts we can give to a grieving person. If we need a few guidelines, there are some helpful do's and don'ts which most grief counselors advise. Don't offer drugs to suppress grief and don't stop people from crying. Do listen and do let a person in grief express whatever he or she is feeling no matter how irrational it might sound—it's therapeutic. Most important, do speak as naturally as you can. You can say you feel terrible because you didn't get to see the person who died the other day, or whatever you are truly feeling. A condolence call is not, however, the best time to talk about your own losses. You have come to discuss the bereaved person's problems, and you can't expect someone in grief to relate to yours at the moment. Further down the road you may want to share your feelings about losses in your own life, but that should be put on the back burner for awhile.

A study by sociologist Marcelle Y. Chenard revealed that a common phrase like "I'm sorry" when repeated over and over again by callers will tend to produce anger in the grieving person. But don't fault yourself when that slips out. If you feel you can't remain silent, then trust your instincts and try to say simply what's in your heart.

117

It would certainly be easier if there were an etiquette of love, but we can only agree with novelist Aldous Huxley that "There isn't any formula or method. You learn to love by loving — by paying attention and thereby discovering what needs to be done."

If we can trust ourselves enough to let go of the rules, to forget about what is socially acceptable and simply be there with another person, we will find the right things to say and do. When we are willing to join with someone who is confronting death and loss, we can tap into our own limitless wellspring of love and find we have just what is needed—a loving presence that heals and lets the grass grow green again.

AFTERWORD

Sooner or later each of us comes to a place in time that is marked by loss and grief. No one can make this passage for us, but other people can certainly lighten the way. The Center, an idea that took root and flowered, is essentially a gathering together to heal. We would be happy to assist those who want to establish their own community support network. In fact, we will be publishing a book on the guidelines that have been most useful for us.

We know the Center's methods have worked for many people, but we believe that the real value lies not so much in form as in content, which is a willingness to come together out of mutual respect, and to support those experiencing loss as they heal in their own way.

If you would like more information on the Center, help finding resources in your own community or information on starting a support system, please contact us:

THE CENTER FOR HELP IN TIME OF LOSS
600 BLUE HILL ROAD
RIVER VALE, NEW JERSEY 07675
(201) 391-4473

REFLECTIONS:

Favorite Readings

from The Center

CARVINGS IN THE CANYON

Sometimes I could feel the wind blowing through my
    soul
Scattering the pieces of the dreams that someone
    stole
The man I called my father, his eyes were all I knew
The man who threw away my love, the child that
    never grew

So I built a wall around my life and sealed off all my
    dreams
And hid behind the silence of my stifled little screams
I knew all love had left me and thought no more
    would be found
But a steady wind kept rising till it turned my life
    around

And so I've come to love the windstorms that blew
    my life apart
Without them there would never be the carvings in
    my heart
And I've come to love the sculptor and the hands
    that move the knife
Through the beauty of the carvings in the canyon of
    my life

The carvings taught me how to love the strangers
    that see
To reach beyond their canyon walls and hold them
    close to me
To know them in their beauty and to know them in
    their pain
And to know with different carvings one heart that
    beats the same

And so I've come to love the sculptor and the hands
    that move the knife

I've come to love the carvings in the canyon of my
    life
I've come through all the windstorms that blew my
    life apart
Through the beauty of the carvings in the canyon of
    my heart

—Words and Music by Barbara Meislin
and Amanda McBroom

Have patience with all things, but first of all with yourself.

—St. Francis de Sales

Look to this day,
For it is life,
The very life of life.
In its brief course lies all
The realities and verities of existence,
The bliss of growth,
The splendor of action,
The glory of power.

For yesterday is but a dream
And tomorrow is only a vision.
But today, well lived,
Makes every yesterday a dream of happiness
And every tomorrow a vision of Hope.

Look well, therefore, to this day.

—Sanskrit Proverb

Here is a poem from the Jewish service of the dead called "Yiskor" which means "Remembrance."

IN MEMORY OF OUR BELOVED CHILDREN

In the rising of the sun
    and in its going down:—
        we remember them.

In the blowing of the wind
    and in the chill of winter:—
        we remember them.

In the opening of buds
    and in the warmth of summer:—
        we remember them.

In the rustling of leaves
    and the beauty of autumn:—
        we remember them.

In the beginning of the year
    and when it ends:—
        we remember them.

For we are weary
    and in need of strength:—
        we remember them.

When we are lost
    and sick at heart:—
        we remember them.

When we have joys we
    yearn to share:—
        we remember them.

So long as we live
They too shall live

For they are now part of us:—
    As we remember them.

IF I HAD MY LIFE TO LIVE OVER

I'd dare to make more mistakes next time.
I'd relax. I would limber up.
I would be sillier than I have been this trip.
I would take fewer things seriously.
I would take more chances. I would take more trips.
I would climb more mountains and swim more rivers.
I would eat more ice-cream and less beans.
I would perhaps have more actual troubles, but I'd
    have fewer imaginary ones.

You see, I'm one of those people who live sensibly
    and sanely
Hour after hour, day after day.
Oh, I've had my moments and if I had it to do over
    again I'd have more of them.
In fact, I'd try to have nothing else.
Just moments
One after another, instead of living so many years
    ahead of each day.
I've been one of those persons who never goes
    anywhere without a thermometer, a hot water
    bottle, a raincoat, and a parachute.
If I had to do it again, I would travel lighter than I
    have.

If I had my life to live over, I would start barefoot
    earlier in the spring
And stay that way later in the fall.
I would go to more dances.
I would ride more merry-go-rounds.
I would pick more daisies.

—*Nadine Stair, age 85*

PLEASE LISTEN!

When I ask you to listen to me and you start giving
advice, you have not done what I asked.

When I ask you to listen to me and you begin to tell
me why I shouldn't feel that way, you are
trampling on my feelings.

When I ask you to listen to me and you feel you have
to do something to solve my problem, you have
failed me, strange as that may seem.

Listen! All I asked was that you listen, not talk or
do—just hear me.

Advice is cheap; *twenty cents* will get you both Dear
Abby and Billy Graham in the same newspaper.

And I can do for myself. I'm not helpless. Maybe
discouraged and faltering, but not helpless.

When you do something for me that I can and need
to do for myself, you contribute to my fear and
inadequacy.

BUT WHEN YOU

*accept as a simple fact that I do feel what I feel, no
matter how irrational,* then I can quit trying to
convince you and can get about this business of
understanding what's behind this irrational feeling.

And when that's clear, the answers are obvious and I
don't need advice. Irrational feelings make sense
when we understand what's behind them.

So please listen and just hear me. And, if you want
to talk, wait a minute for your turn, and I'll listen
to you.

—Dr. Ray Houghton
(Copied from Trinity Reformed Chimes)

Genuine insight may be needed for self-understanding—but naked courage is required for self-love. In a sense—it is not enough to simply understand, interpret or explain; what gives our thoughts life—and our life, love? Courage—the courage to let go of our guilt and self torture—the courage to decide in favor of ourselves—to be gentle—to love ourselves. St. Paul has written: "If God is for us, who can be against us?" My friends, it is time to surrender within.

I may be able to speak
with great wisdom and understanding
but if I do not love myself,
then I understand nothing.

I may talk a good game
I might know a lot about life
but if I do not know that I am loved—
then I know nothing.

I may be a person of strong faith
be able to believe with certainty
but if I do not believe in myself—
then I believe in nothing.

I may be a person who is always giving,
always caring about others' needs—
but if I do this, because I can't
allow myself to need—
then my caring is crippled—
it does me no good.

I love myself when I am patient
when I can be quiet with waiting—
not rushing my joy
nor denying my pain.

I am my own friend—
with kindness for free—
I own what I am
    my anger and hurt
    my laughter and love
they never own me.

Although my life may be fragile
    with failure—
I am not afraid
I do not hold on to what has gone
    wrong—
for me living is now and
    love is today.

—*Charles Lochner*

PERSPECTIVE

I am standing on the seashore. A ship spreads her sails to the morning breeze and starts for the ocean.

I stand watching her until she fades on the horizon, and someone at my side says, "She is gone!"

"Gone where?"

The loss of sight is in me, not in her.

Just at the moment when someone says, "She is gone!" there are others watching her coming. Others voices take up the glad shout, "Here she comes!"

And that is dying.

—*Henry Scott Holland*

COMES THE DAWN

After a while you learn the subtle difference
Between holding a hand and chaining a soul,
And you learn that love doesn't mean leaning,
And company doesn't mean security,
And you begin to learn that kisses aren't contracts
And presents aren't promises,
And you begin to accept your defeats
With your head up and your eyes open,
With the grace of a woman, not the grief of a child.
And you learn to build all your roads
On today because tomorrow's ground
Is too uncertain for plans, and futures have
A way of falling down in mid-flight.
After a while you learn that even sunshine
Burns if you get too much.
So you plant your own garden and decorate
Your own soul, instead of waiting
For someone to bring you flowers.
And you learn that you really can endure . . .
That you really are strong
And you really do have worth.

And you learn and learn . . .
With every good-bye you learn.

—Author unknown

Somehow we think it's not all right to feel bad. The next
book I write is going to be called "I'm not O.K. and
You're not O.K., and That's O.K."

—Elisabeth Kübler-Ross, M.D.

Be patient toward all that is unresolved
    in your heart
Try to love the questions themselves. . .

Do not now seek the answers
    which cannot be given
    because you would not be able
    to live them
And the point is,
    to live everything.

Live the questions now
Perhaps you will then
    gradually,
    without noticing it,
Live along some distant day
    into the answers.

— Rainer Maria Rilke

IN SEARCH OF SEASONS

The seasons within you come and
    go,
And who you are you do not know.

Your dreams must memorize the
    course
To lead you to a higher source.

You are the flower, you are the
    force.
You reap the harvest, shed the
    snow.

You are the one. You are the
    whole.
You are the seasons of your soul.

— BettyClare Moffatt

WHEREVER YOU GO

I want to say something
    to all of you, who
    have become a part of
    the fabric of my life.

The color and texture
    which you have brought into my being
    have become a song
    and I want to sing it forever.

There is an energy in us
    which makes things happen when
    the paths of other persons touch ours
    and we have to be there and let it happen.

When the time
    of our particular sunset comes,
    "Our Thing," our accomplishment,
    won't matter a great deal.

But the clarity and care
    with which we have loved others
    will speak with vitality of the great gift of Life
    we have been for each other.

— written and sung by
The Monks of the Weston Priory
from Weston, Vt.

Back of tranquility
lies always conquered
unhappiness.

— Eleanor Roosevelt

YOUR SONG

Sometimes
sometimes at night
I sit and wonder
about your soul
& sometimes
sometimes I wonder
if you were set free
would you live in the mountains
and speak through the wind
will you whisk through my hair
and sometimes
you might be the rain
& mix with my tears
of memories we share.
I hope you remember
this life before death
I hope you remember
your life was worth living
I hope you enjoy
your life after life.

And sometimes
whenever it's raining
whenever the wind caresses my hair
I'll smile and know you are with me
and life will light up my eyes
and thank you
     thank you for living.

— Les Alexander

There comes a time in a man's life
when to get where he has to go —
if there are no doors or windows he
walks through a wall.

— Bernard Malamud

COME HOME

Come home.
The tower waits.
The sea is still.
Dark gone. Light breaks.
Do what you will.

Serene, the tower.
Serene, the waiting sea.
Come home
Alone
Wherever you may be.

The hour creates the hour
I come to tell you.
Only
Come home
To filling sea,
To towers that will not fall
To infinity.
I come to tell you of that energy.

And of that high and holy power
        within
Your own serene and inner citadel.
Come home.

                                —*BettyClare Moffatt*

In the depth of winter,
I finally learned that within
me there lay an invincible
summer.

                        — *Albert Camus*

LET GO AND LET GOD

As children bring their broken toys,
With tears for us to mend,
I brought my broken dreams to God
Because He was my friend.

But then instead of leaving Him
In peace to work alone,
I hung around and tried to help
With ways that were my own.

At last, I snatched them back and cried
"How can you be so slow?"
"My child," He said, "What could I do?
"You never did let go."

— *Anonymous*

I want to be thoroughly used up when I die, for the harder I work, the more I live. I rejoice in life for its own sake. Life is no "brief candle" to me. It is a sort of splendid torch which I have got hold of for the moment, and I want to make it burn as brightly as possible before handing it on to future generations.

— *George Bernard Shaw*

Quiet minds cannot be perplexed
or frightened, but go on in fortune or
misfortune at their own private pace,
like a clock in a thunder storm.

— *Robert Louis Stevenson*

A friend is one
    to whom one may pour
out all the contents
    of one's heart,
chaff and grain together
    knowing that the
gentlest of hands
    will take and sift it,
keep what is worth keeping
    and with a breath of kindness
blow the rest away.

— Arabian proverb

Do not stand at my grave and weep:
I am not there. I do not sleep.
I am a thousand winds that blow.
I am the diamond glints on snow.
I am the sunlight on ripened grain.
I am the gentle autumn rain.
When you awaken in the morning's hush,
    I am the swift uplifting rush - of quiet birds in circled
flight,
I am the soft stars that shine at night.
Do not stand at my grave and cry;
I am not there, I did not die.

— Author unknown

BEREAVEMENT SUPPORT RESOURCES

For a complete list of *Friends of Elisabeth Kubler-Ross* support groups and contact people throughout the United States and the world, write to:

Elisabeth Kubler-Ross Center
S. Route 616
Headwaters, VA 24442
(703) 396-3441

Self-Help Clearinghouses provide information about all types of Mutual Aid Self-Help Groups. The following states have self-help clearinghouses:

California 1-800-222-LINK (in CA only)
Connecticut (203) 789-7645
Illinois 1-800-322-MASH (in IL)
Kansas (316) 686-1205
Massachusetts (413) 545-2313
Michigan 1-800-752-5858 (in MI)
Minnesota (612) 642-4060
Missouri (816) 361-5007
Nebraska (402) 476-9668
New Jersey 1-800-FOR-MASH
New York (518) 474-6293
Oregon (503) 222-5555
Pennsylvania (412) 247-5400
South Carolina (803) 791-2426
Texas (214) 871-2420
Vermont 1-800-442-5356

For national U.S. listings and directories:

Self-Help Clearinghouse NJ   (201) 625-7101
Self-Help Center IL   (312) 328-0470
National Clearinghouse NY   (212) 840-1259

Local bereavement resources can often be found by calling your:

Chamber of Commerce
United Way
Town or City Hall
Hospice
Hospital
Church
Synagogue

CHILD LOSS
The following organizations have chapters nationwide and/or can provide important information and support for grieving parents.

Compassionate Friends   For parents and siblings
P.O. Box 1347   grieving the death of
Oak Brook, IL 60521   a child.
(312) 990-0010

Parents of Murdered Children
1739 Bella Vista
Cincinnati, OH
(513) 242-8025

National Sudden Infant Death Syndrome Foundation
310 S. Michigan Ave.
Chicago, IL 60604
(312) 663-0650

National Foundation for Sudden Infant Death
1501 Broadway
New York, NY 10036
(800) 638-7437

Bereaved Families of Ontario
214 Merton St.
Toronto, Ontario
M4S 1A6

The following organizations are for parents who have experienced miscarriage, stillbirth, or loss of a newborn.

Unite, Inc.
c/o Jeanes Hospital
7600 Central Ave.
Philadelphia, PA 19111
(215) 728-2082

A.M.E.N.D.
Maureen Connelly
4324 Berrywick Terrace
St. Louis, MO 63128
(314) 487-7582

S.H.A.R.E.
St. John's Hospital
800 E. Carpenter
Springfield, IL 62769
(217) 544-6464 ext. 5275

SUPPORT FOR WIDOWED PERSONS

Theos
Suite 306
Office Building
Penn Hills Mall
Pittsburgh, PA 15235
(412) 243-4299

This group has a spiritual emphasis and maintains 100 chapters nationwide.

Widowed Persons Service
1909 K Street NW
Washington, D.C.
(202) 872-4700

Society of
Military Widows
P.O. Box 1714
La Mesa, CA 92041

For survivors of career military men.

Young Widow/
Widower Support
Group
Dr. Reuben
(215) 338-9934

Meets in Philadelphia.

T.L.A.
(To Live Again), Inc.
P.O. Box 103
West Chester, PA 19380

Pennsylvania and Delaware area only.

Parents Without
Partners
7910 Woodmont Ave.
Bethesda, MD 20014
(301) 654-8850

This group primarily for divorced people maintains 1,000 chapters nationwide and some have special discussion groups for widowed people.

SUICIDE

Following are national headquarters of suicide survivor support groups.

Survivors Helping Survivors
Marcia Williams
Emergency Dept.
St. Luke's Hospital
2900 W. Oklahoma Ave.
Milwuakee, WI 53215

Ray of Hope, Inc.
P.O. Box 2323
Iowa City, Iowa 52244

Students Against Suicide   Teens working to
P.O. Box 115   prevent teen suidicide.
S. Laguna, CA 92677
(714) 496-4566

Survivors of Suicide
Sharry Schaefer
3251 N. 78th St.
Milwaukee, WI 53222
(414) 442-4638

M.A.P. (Mother of AIDS Patients)
P.O. Box 1763
Lomita, CA 90717

A national network for families of AIDS patients and survivors of those who have died of AIDS. Offers group and individual counseling and a hotline service, numbers listed below.

Joyce Brink	(213) 329-8697
Barbara Cleaver	(213) 530-2109
Helencare Cox	(818) 794-1455
Mary Jane Edwards	(213) 541-3134
Janet McMahon	(213) 542-3019
Bea Simon	(213) 661-1954

SUGGESTED READINGS

AIDS: A Self-Care Manual. AIDS Project Los Angeles, Betty-Clare Moffatt, et. al., eds. Santa Monica, California: IBS Press, 1987.

The Bereaved Parent. Harriet Sarnoff Schiff. New York: Crown Books, 1987.

Birth to Birth, The Life Death Mystery. Rev. Gerald P. Ruane. New York: Alba House, 1976.

The Book: On the Taboo Against Knowing Who You Are. Alan Watts. New York: Vintage Books, a Division of Random House, 1966.

Children and Death. Elisabeth Kubler-Ross, M.D. New York: Collier Books, Macmillan & Co. Publishing, 1985.

Compassion and Self-Hate, An Alternative to Despair. Theodore Isaac Rubin, M.D. New York: Ballantine Books, 1975.

Creative Divorce. Mel Krantzler. New York: M. Evans & Co., Inc., 1973.

Death and the Family. L. Pincus. New York: Pantheon Books, 1974.

Death Be Not Proud. John Gunther. New York: Harper & Row, 1949.

Death, The Final Stage of Growth. Elisabeth Kubler-Ross, M.D. Englewood Cliffs, New Jersey: Prentice Hall, 1975.

Explaining Death to Children. Earl Grollman. Boston, Massachusetts: Beacon Press, 1967.

Gifts for the Living: Conversations with Caregivers on Death and Dying. BettyClare Moffatt. Santa Monica, California: IBS Press, 1988.

Good Grief, A Constructive Appproach to the Problem of Loss. Granger F. Westberg. Philadelphia, Pennsylvania: Fortress Press, 1962.

Good-bye to Guilt. Releasing Fear Through Forgiveness. Gerald G. Jampolsky, M.D. New York: Bantam Books, 1985.

Man's Search for Meaning. Viktor E. Frankl. New York: Pocket Books, A Division of Simon & Schuster, 1959.

The Many Faces of Grief. Edgar N. Jackson. Nashville, Tennesee: Abingdon Press, 1972.

A New Age Handbook on Death and Dying. Carol Parrish-Harra. Santa Monica, California: IBS Press, 1988.

On Death and Dying. Elisabeth Kubler-Ross, M.D. New York: Macmillan, 1969.

Questions On Death and Dying. Elisabeth Kubler-Ross. New York: MacMillan, 1974.

Someone You Love Is Dying (A Guide for Helping & Coping). Martin Shepard, M.D. New York: Harmony Books, a Division of Crown Publishing, 1975.

A Sorrow Beyond Dreams: A Life Story. Peter Handke. London: Souvenir Press, 1976.

A Spirituality Named Compassion. Mathew Fox. San Francisco, California: Winston Press, A Division of Harper & Row, 1979.

Unconditional Love and Forgiveness. Edith R. Stauffer. Burbank, California: Triangle Publishers, 1987.

When Someone You Love Has AIDS: A Book of Hope for Family and Friends. BettyClare Moffatt. New York: NAL Books, 1987.

Widow. Lynne Caine. New York: Bantam Books, 1974.

The Woman Said Yes. Jessamyn West. New York: Harcourt, Brace, Jovanovich, 1976.

Word and Image. C.G. Jung. Ed. by Aniela Jaffe. Princeton, New Jersey: Bollingen Series XC VII:2, Princeton University Press, 1979.

You and Your Grief. Edgar N. Jackson. New York: Hawthorn Books, 1961.

PROFESSIONAL CAREGIVERS BIBLIOGRAPHY

Anticipatory Grief. Bernard Schoenberg, et. al., eds. New York: Columbia University Press, 1974.

Attachment and Loss, Vol. 2: Separation: Anxiety and Anger. J. Bowlby. New York: Basic Books, Inc., 1973.

Attachment and Loss, Vol 3: Loss, Sadness and Depression. J. Bowlby. New York: Basic Books, Inc., 1980.

Bereavement: Its Psychosocial Aspects. Bernard Schoenberg et. al., eds. New York: Columbia University Press, 1975.

Bereavement: Studies of Grief in Adult Life. Colin Murray Parkes. New York: International Universities Press, 1972.

The Courage to Grieve: Creative living, Recovery and Growth Through Grief. J. Tatelbaum. New York: Harper Row, 1980.

Deaths of Man. Edwin S. Schneidman. Baltimore, Md: Penguin Books, 1973.

Ethical Issues in Death and Dying. Robert F. Weir. New York: Columbia University Press, 1977.

The First Year of Bereavement. Glick, Weiss, and Parkes. New York: John Wiley & Sons, Inc., 1974.

The Grief Process: Analysis and Counseling. Yorick Spiegel. Nashville, Tenn: Abingdon Press, 1973.

The Healing Power of Grief. Jack S. Miller. New York: Seabury Press, 1978.

Helping Each Other in Widowhood. P.R. Silverman, et. al. New York: Heneth Science Publishing Co., 1974.

Learning to Say Goodbye When A Parent Dies. E. Le Shan. New York: MacMillan, 1976.

Loss and Grief: Psychological Movement in Medical Practice. Bernard Schoenberg et. al., eds. New York: Columbia University Press, 1970.

New Meanings of Death. Herman Feifel, ed. New York: McGraw Hill, 1959.

"Recent Bereavement as a Cause of Mental Illness." *British Journal of Psychiatry,* 110:198-204, 1964.

"Symptomology and Management of Acute Grief." *American Journal of Psychiatry,* 101: 7-21, September 1944.

I would like to share this information with others...

QUANTITY	BOOK TITLES	PRICE	TOTAL
	STEPPING STONES TO GRIEF RECOVERY —Deborah Roth	$8.95	
	GIFTS FOR THE LIVING: Conversations With Care-givers on Death and Dying —BettyClare Moffatt, et. al.	9.95	
	A NEW AGE HANDBOOK ON DEATH AND DYING —Carol Parrish-Harra	8.95	
	AIDS: A SELF-CARE MANUAL* —AIDS Project Los Angeles (320 pp.)	12.95	
	WHEN SOMEONE YOU LOVE HAS AIDS: A Book of Hope for Family & Friends —BettyClare Moffatt	8.95	
	SHIPPING & HANDLING ($2.00 for first book, $1.00 each additional book)		
	SALES TAX 6.5% (California residents only)		
	TOTAL DUE		

Please send check or money order to:

IBS PRESS
744 Pier Avenue
Santa Monica, CA 90405
(213) 450-6485

Name_____

Address_____

City/State/Zip_____

* Quantity discounts are available to AIDS-related organizations.